JAPAN IN 22 DAYS

A STEP-BY-STEP-GUIDE AND TRAVEL ITINERARY

BY DAVID OLD

Dedicated to my father, W. T. Old Jr., first but not last of the Olds to love Japan.
Also dedicated to the Fort Lewis College Japan Group of '75. What a bunch!
Also to my new and excellent school, the College of Santa Fe, where Brothers Arthur and Andre have treated me so well and patiently. Thanks also to Maria who has listened so pleasantly to my verbal rambling.
Special mention to my Japanophile friends the Essermans and to the Trumans who have stuck it out the longest in Kobe.
All my love to the Morikawa family of Neyagawa City and their friends who have suffered so long with their "henna Gaijin" son. And of course, I love you the mostest Mom.
Last yet far from least, all my love and thanks to Zoe, whose love, laundry, lunches and long-suffering make all my escapades possible, pleasant and worthwhile.
God bless you all. Live long, prosper and visit more often.

Copyright © 1987 by David Old
Cover and maps copyright © 1987 by John Muir Publications

Library of Congress Catalog No. 87-042774

Published by John Muir Publications
Santa Fe, New Mexico
Printed in U.S.A.

Editor Richard Harris
Design/Production Mary Shapiro
Maps Deborah Reade
Cover Map Tim Clark
Typography Copygraphics, Inc., Santa Fe, NM

ISBN 0-912528-73-7

CONTENTS

How to Use This Book 6
Basic Travel Methods 13
Itinerary 22
DAY 1 Depart USA—Tokyo 27
DAY 2 Explore Tokyo 34
DAY 3 More of Tokyo 37
DAY 4 Izu Peninsula—Shimoda—Toi 41
DAY 5 Toi and Matsuzaki 45
DAY 6 Ise 46
DAY 7 Ise—Kyoto 49
DAY 8 Kyoto 53
DAY 9 Kyoto—Nara 58
DAY 10 Himeji and Kotohira 61
DAY 11 Miyajima 65
DAY 12 Miyajima 68
DAY 13 Hiroshima—Travel to Kyushu 70
DAY 14 Yobuko Town—Hatomizaki 75
DAY 15 Hatomizaki—Kyoto 78
DAY 16 Travel to Hakui 79
DAY 17 Travel to Sado Island 81
DAY 18 Sado 83
DAY 19 Sado to Bandai 86
DAY 20 Travel to Nikko 89
DAY 21 Chuzenji/Nikko 92
DAY 22 Nikko—Tokyo 94
Post-Tour Option Hokkaido 96
Food 106
History 113
Language 118
Youth Hostels 128
Festivals 130
Directory 132

Japan in 22 Days

HOW TO USE THIS BOOK

This book is the tour guide in your pocket, a tried and proven plan to see Japan in a few short weeks. It gives you the travel efficiency of an organized tour plus do-it-yourself freedom and flexibility.

Japan in 22 Days tells you how to get the most out of Japan's super-modern Bullet Trains using a rail pass that's only available to foreigners (that's us). Ferries, local trains and buses will take you deep into the countryside where American tourists are rare and the English language might as well be Navajo. You'll eat and sleep Japanese-style in traditional country inns known as minshuku and ryokan.

This book is a selective, not comprehensive, travel guide. The Japanese like to group their sightseeing highlights by threes: "One of the nation's three most beautiful gardens" (or islands, or waterfalls). In this itinerary I won't take you to all three gardens, only the best of the three. Which one is "best," of course, is my personal opinion—based on fifteen trips to Japan, a total of over twenty-four months traveling, studying and living there. Besides Japan's "bests" and "most beautifuls," I'll show you some totally unique places that other guidebooks never mention—including my favorite picnic spot.

Efficient travelers think ahead. Read the whole book as you plan the trip. Modify the plan to suit your schedule and interests. If you want to see a place that's not in the itinerary, rearrange the itinerary. My tour connects destinations by the easiest routes, so if you want to break off, wait until you get in the general neighborhood.

Once you've started the trip, It may be difficult to alter your plans without missing accommodations you've reserved and perhaps prepaid. Lodging reservations are much more important in Japan (especially away from big cities) than in most western nations. Even the youth hostel style National Citizens' Hotels are often booked up months in advance.

The itinerary format I've used in this book is divided into 22 daily sections, containing:

1. A **general overview** of each day.

2. A **suggested schedule** for travel, sightseeing, shopping and meals.

3. A list of major **sightseeing highlights**. These are rated in order of importance: ▲▲▲ Don't miss; ▲▲ Try hard to see; and ▲ See if you get a chance.

4. **Transportation**—trains, buses and ferries, how to find them and when to go.

How to Use This Book 7

    5. **Food and lodging**—where to find the best of each.
    6. **Helpful hints**, random informational tidbits that will help your day go better.
    7. Clear, user-friendly **maps**. To get the most out of them, learn the following symbols:

At the back of the book you will find information covering language, food, history and festivals. Read these last pages along with the first. A Hokkaido **post-tour option** is there for people who just can't get enough.

Nobody Does It Better

In *Japan in 22 Days* I present what I personally consider to be an ideal plan for touring Japan—but let's face it, I'm not you. Read every piece of information you can lay your hands on ahead of time, customize this itinerary and design your own perfect trip. A self-guided tour has many advantages, but it also means you do the work of the tour company, making advance arrangements which, in Japan, are especially important. The Japanese national character is fanatically organized, so touring the country requires more organization than other parts of the world.

Very few Japanese travel without reservations, so innkeepers expect them. You can turn up out of the blue and still find a place to stay if necessary, but the more reservations you have and can stick to, the easier your trip will be. You can travel at will, unhindered, but most people do better sticking to a schedule for comfort's sake. By reserving ahead you will also save your Japanese hosts a lot of anxiety by informing them that they should expect a Gaijin (foreigner) under their roof. Remember that once off the beaten path, non-Japanese faces can be rare. The more you plan and organize ahead, the smoother, easier and more enjoyable your tour will be.

Lay out your own travel plan following the book itinerary when convenient. If you would rather see more of Kyoto instead of going on to an out-of-the-way (and beautiful) island or castle, by all means join up with the book a day or two later. Just plan ahead to avoid confusion.

When to Go

Japan covers as many lines of latitude as the U.S., so picking an ideal time to go can be tough. Unless you're going skiing, Hokkaido would be a bad choice in the winter, just as nearly all the rest of the country is very hot from late June to August. Fortunately, the locals take their main national holiday from the end of July to the middle of August. I say "main" holiday because they take many other vacations throughout the year. For example, if you plan to be in the Inland Sea during cherry blossom time, you will absolutely need reservations.

Spring and fall are the best times to travel, but other times have their advantages as well. Tokyo can be gorgeous at dawn in December. The warmth of Kyushu's beaches is only a morning's train ride from a frigid, foggy Kyoto morning. If you could only go in winter you could focus more on the hot springs which abound all over the country. You would see Mt. Fuji at it's finest: snow-capped. The island of Sado would be a definite miss unless you have a passion for violent sea storms. (They're astonishing!) On the other hand, you could live in the beautiful clear waters around Sado in July or August.

Spring and fall are best; any other time of year runs a close second.

Cost

Yes, the land of the rising yen is expensive. The cost of rooms and transportation is as high as almost anywhere else in the world (unless you consider Aspen, Las Vegas or Disney World). But you'll feel you've gotten more than your money's worth when you return home. You'll have far more than just photos and souvenirs to show for your trip: you will have experienced one of the world's most unique and influential cultures.

$2500 apiece will do the trick for airfare, rail pass, lodging and meals. This figure allows just $200 for "glad money," but you'll lodge in quality ryokan and minshuku. You could economize and lower the cost to about $2000 if necessary, by staying in youth hostels where available (see the listing in the back of the book), avoiding car rentals and taxis, and cutting corners on lunches and nightlife. The money I suggest you spend will ease you into Japan as an average citizen. The richness of the experience will be worth a lot more than the dent your wallet, I promise.

Recommended Reading
If possible, before you leave home go to your local bookstore and purchase a selection of the following books:

Dictionaries and Language Books: A small vest-pocket English-Japanese/Japanese-English dictionary is best. Be sure to pick one with the Japanese portions written in the Roman alphabet (which the Japanese call Romaji), not Kanji (Chinese-style) ideograms. A table that translates Japanese Hirigana and Katakana alphabets into their Romaji phonetic equivalents is helpful if you want to try deciphering Japanese words on signs or brochures.

Among the best pocket-sized books for learning to read Japanese is *Everyday Japanese Characters* by Michael Pye, published by Hokuseido Press, Tokyo, distributed in the U.S. by Heian International, Inc., P.O. Box 2402, South San Francisco, CA 94080.

A phrasebook is only useful if you really intend to study the language. You can ask questions with a phrasebook, but will you understand the answers? I've included some phrases in the back of this book, and most dictionaries have a phrase section. There are plenty of phrasebooks for sale in Japan if you should feel yourself desperately in need of one.

The best books for English-speakers to gain insight into subtleties of Japanese language and culture are a series of slim volumes called *Nihongo Notes* by Osamu Mizutani and Nobuko Mizutani, published by The Japan Times, Ltd., and widely available in Japan. These books (*Speaking and Living in Japan, Expressing Oneself in Japanese, Understanding Communication in Japanese*, etc.) are compiled from a daily column in *The Japan Times*, an excellent English-language newspaper found in most Japanese cities.

Guidebooks: Purchase a comprehensive guidebook as a companion to this one. Of the many on the market, the familiar Fodor's and Baedecker's remain, in my opinion, the best. *Japan in 22 Days* provides an itinerary for a true insider's look at Japan. It's the skeleton on which you hang the muscle and add the character. I won't tell you why the Daibutsu, the great Buddha, holds his fingers like that. Fodor's will.

Each guidebook has its own distinctive format and style. Browse through them at the bookstore and find one that you'd like to live with for a month. If you leave home without a guidebook, you'll find a good selection in Maruzen and Kinokuniya bookstores in major Japanese cities.

Some of the best places we'll visit on this itinerary are only mentioned briefly (or not at all) in most "comprehensive" guidebooks. Supplement your library with the English-language info readily available at Japan's Tourist Information Centers.

General Background Reading: The best general information book on Japan is *Japan: A Traveler's Companion*, by Lensey Namioka, published by Vanguard Press, New York, ISBN 8146-0816-0. It covers a great variety of subjects in a clear, understandable style.

Edwin O. Reishauer's book *The Japanese*, from Belknap Press (Harvard University), is considered the definitive work.

A painless way to learn about Japanese culture, customs and history is to spend spare moments both before and during your trip reading a novel set in Japan. A couple of suggestions . . .

Lafcadio Hearn wrote of turn-of-the century Japan in a series of short story collections, novels and essays of which the most readily available is *Writings from Japan* (Penguin Books).

Works by two of Japan's greatest 20th century literary figures, Mishima Yukio (*The Sea of Fertility Tetralogy*, *The Sailor Who Fell from Grace with the Sea*) and Yasumari Kawabata (*Beauty and Sadness*, *The Master of Go*, and *Snow Country* which takes place in a traditional Japanese inn) are available in inexpensive paperback English language translations. For an eyewitness account of Japanese culture before its first contact with the western world, read the medieval epic *The Tale of Genji* ("'Genji Monogatari'") by Lady Murasaki Shikibu, currently available from Knopf and found in most U.S. libraries. The romantic treatment will enhance present day reality.

The Japan National Tourist Bureau (JTB), will send you lots of good literature free for the asking. Their addresses and telephone numbers are in the appendix or major metropolitan phone books.

Your traveling library should also include a copy of *Asia Through the Back Door* by Rick Steves and John Gottberg (from John Muir Publications, 1987-88 revised edition $11.95). Asia's a big place, and only a small part of the book relates directly to Japan. But Rick Steves (who also pioneered the "22 Days" itinerary-guidebook format) and John Gottberg (former editor of "Insight Guides") have a remarkable sense of the practical problems American travelers face in Asia. Their book provides sound advice on subjects ranging from travel photography to laundry, and encourages a mental attitude that makes all the difference in experiencing and enjoying Asia's very foreign cultures.

Don't Panic!
Speaking of mental attitude: Before my first trip to Japan, as one of a group of 24 college students, our group leader made us read a short article on "culture shock" —an emotional rejection of a culture based on subconscious fear (xenophobia) laced with homesickness.

After the first weeks of homestay life with Japanese families in the industrial environs of Osaka, all the members of our group found ourselves in a constant state of mental malaise. The reasons? Everything from curfew at our Japanese homes, to too damn much Japanese food. Jim, our leader, called a group meeting one afternoon after school and told us point-blank that we were all suffering from "culture shock." Ah, Baloney!, we cried as one . but then, words faintly remembered from the article he'd made us read came drifting back.

"Criminey!" I thought, "I'm acting like the ignorant specimen I vowed never to be." Honestly, folks, recognizing the problem was all it took to get every one of us back on track. Soon we were enjoying Japan and our homestay families like never before.

If you wake up one morning seething mad because you've been served sea slug for breakfast once too often, remember: your hosts think you like sea slug! You have only to explain that you would really rather have a fried egg and toast, and you'll get it.

In this three-week trip, you'll see more of Japan then the average so called Japanologist does in his one or two year stay. To absorb and fully enjoy it requires a willingness to see, feel and experience without comparing it to "back home." (There will be plenty of time later to compare aspects of your everyday life to what you discovered in Japan.) The Japanese *are* different, as we are to them—sometimes maddeningly so. Relax. Somehow they've managed just fine for thousands of years, and rest assured they'll keep right on doing so after you've gone.

The more you can let go and get into the culture, the more you'll get out of the experience. If you read up beforehand, you'll waste less energy being astounded by new behavior and you'll be better able to experience and appreciate it.

Learn a few words of Japanese. Sure, it's a fairly difficult language, but so what? Don't worry about your accent—just say it. People from Tokyo poke fun at the merchants' accent from Osaka, too; the typical Osaka greeting, "Mo karemaka?" ("Making any money?") is good for a laugh most places outside of Osaka.

A simple greeting in Japanese will loosen up everyone in the little bar or teashop you happen into. Remember that many Japanese, particularly in the countryside, *have never seen a foreigner*! Don't be excessively noisy, but don't be shy either.

If you catch the fellow at the end of the bar staring at you, don't get upset—talk to him. He's curious, not rude. He knows about Gaijin (foreigners) mainly from TV and print media— usually as beautiful models enjoying the good life and selling something. Now, into his local coffee shop steps the real thing. Wouldn't you be curious? Dare to communicate with him!

BASIC TRAVEL METHODS

Packing

What to carry along is the eternal question for travelers. If you could travel in the "old style" it would be no problem. You would have several steamer trunks full of all that life might require and armies of helpful bearers to lug it all around for you. No such luck in modern Japan, though. All the money in the world won't get you a porter on a crowded morning in Ueno Station. Japan is a very egalitarian sort of place when it comes to luggage—every man for himself (women, too).

You'll often see Japanese people, masters at the art of packing light, who set out on long journeys with a bare minimum of belongings. Personally, I prefer the luxury of a few changes of clothing. A fine balance is called for: enough stuff to wear and be comfortable without creating an un-luggable burden.

I strongly recommend convertible luggage that can be carried as a back pack or as a suitcase. The shoulder straps and hip harness typically zip inside when you want to carry the bag by its handle. It's much easier to carry forty pounds on your back than in your hand, yet when checking into a nice hotel or ryokan, you can zip up the straps, leave the vagabond look out on the sidewalk, and check in with dignity. Look for sturdy construction, a main compartment that opens wide so you don't have to 'stuff' your clothes, and a good backpack suspension system. How many external pockets you want is up to you. I carry a bag on which the large outside pocket zips off and becomes a day pack, perfect for carrying my portable computer around in. Good convertible luggage is available from Rick Steves' Back Door Travel in Edmunds, Washington, (206) 771-8303, or from R.E.I. in Seattle, (206) 575-3287. Call for catalogues. The R.E.I. catalogue is also a great source for rain gear, socks, shoes and other items you may need for your trip.

When packing, consider the time of year you'll be going. The only thing you'll use a heavy sweater for in the summer is a pillow.

My Dad's favorite saying was, "Travel light and carry enough money to buy what you need when you get there." This philosophy has its drawbacks, though. While you can get most anything you need in Japan, men especially will have a hard time finding large sizes in clothing and shoes. A Japanese size "LL" (extra large) is a U.S. "Medium." Size 10 shoes are virtually nonexistent.

Obviously you'll find items like toothpaste, shampoo and soap everywhere. Try new brands. The Japanese have some of the best cosmetics in the world.

Carry any prescription medicines you may need in sufficient quantity for the trip and a bit extra. If you wear contacts, carry spares (although I understand Japan is the place to buy good contacts). Any personal hygiene items you are particularly fond of should be carried along, although you will be able to find substitutes if necessary.

Take a couple of small plastic bottles, available at camping stores, to keep soap and detergent in. You will be doing your own laundry often as not. In the cities it is easy enough to find laundries, but out in the country, you'll be using the facilities offered by the inns where you're staying.

Carry more socks than you think you'll ever need.

Carry fewer "dress-up" clothes than you think you need. Carry some nice evening clothes, but be casual. Your hosts won't expect you to have a tux or evening gown.

Carry one or at most two pairs of shoes. Try and find an attractive walking shoe you could bear to go out at night in, too. Rockport High-Tec Walkers, the best traveling shoe I've found, are available from many good quality shoe stores or from Eddie Bauer.

Carry a good *light* raincoat. Not a London Fog; a coated nylon raincoat. Rain in Japan differs from ours. It's soft and warm except in winter, requiring minimal protection. Everyone uses umbrellas, cheap and readily available at umbrella racks everywhere.

Use layers of clothing for cold weather versatility. Unless you plan to go to Hokkaido in winter, skip the down parka. On the other hand, a down vest packs tiny and is great in an emergency cold spell.

Take along a small cheap compass to help you follow maps and directions in this book. A small Swiss Army knife with a can opener, tweezers and tooth pick is invaluable (my favorite model is called the Tinker; it has what you need and no extras).

Pack early—days early. Think about distributing your load so that it will carry nicely and you can find things without groping through your laundry all the time. Pick up your kit and walk a half mile with it. Can you do it? If not, lighten the load. You will get in better shape during the trip, and what seemed heavy at the beginning will seem light at the end; but start light so you can add goodies en-route, avoiding the effort and expense of mailing purchases home from overseas.

Getting There

Korean Air Lines is by far the cheapest way to go. Reserve as far in advance as possible to get the best rates.

Travel Wholesalers International, Inc., a discount ticket broker at Two Skyline Place, 5203 Leesburg Pike, Falls Church

Va. 22041, 800-446-2424 (From Virginia, 800-572-1717), sells KAL tickets at very good prices. A typical Y class (coach) from the west coast is $580.00 round trip. ($710.00 from the east coast.) Business class is around $1400.00 round trip from the west coast.

Lodging

Unless you want to risk traveling unreserved (it can be done, but not always easily), make reservations in advance through the **Tokyo Minshuku Center**, the only organization that will reserve you rooms across the country in the small family-run minshuku and pensions I recommend in this book. Asano-san, the director of the Center, speaks English quite well. He is familiar with *Japan in 22 Days* and can help you select good alternates if any of the inns I recommend are booked up. Send him a clearly written itinerary at least a month in advance of your arrival, and you will have all your reservations in hand by the second day of your trip, if not before you even leave home. The address is: Tokyo Minshuku Center, Kotsu Kaikan Bldg. 2-10-1 Yurakucho, Chiyoda-ku, Tokyo. Ph# (03) 216-6556.

Most of my lodging recommendations fall into two categories, both of which will also provide your morning and evening meals:

Ryokan: Traditional Japanese inns which observe and respect the virtues and beauties of old Japan. The building may not be much to look at from outside, the lobby may be somewhat modern in style, but the spirit will always be traditional. You will often be greeted by a wetted entryway to show welcome. Your room will have tatami mats on the floor, a tokonoma (alcove) for flowers, and austere decoration in the traditional manner. The futons (beds), stored in a closet, will be made for you in the evening, usually while you are in the o-furo (bath) or taking a stroll after dinner in your room. Bathrooms may be in the room but more often, in reasonably priced ryokan, they will be down the hall. There is usually a separate area for brushing teeth and face washing. You will often have a lady in waiting, dressed in kimono, to serve you. Typical ryokan food is kaiseki ryori (see the section on Food), served in your room or in a dining room downstairs.

Minshuku: Minshuku ordinarily cost less than ryokan (though the rates for both vary widely in different areas of the country), and have less personalized service. There's little difference between an *exceptionally good* minshuku and an *average* ryokan. Sometimes the minshuku will be the nicer place; the ones on the Izu Peninsula for example, are very fine and offer a degree of comfort and service unmatched by many ryokan that cost much more. In minshuku you eat in a common dining room instead of the privacy of your own room, and you make up your own bed in the evening. Be polite and pick up your futon in the morning. If you have trouble making the bed or just don't know how, say "Futon o oshienasai" (literally, "Show me the futon'"—not great Japanese, but it will get the idea across).

Note: All prices are quoted per person, with two meals, except at the New Otani Hotel. You may find that you don't like Japanese breakfasts. If so, you can save from 500 to 1000 yen daily by telling the innkeeper, "Asa gohan wa irimasen," I won't be having breakfast. Generally it is easier to just request toast and coffee. It will be cheaper than eating breakfast out.

When staying in either minshuku or ryokan, please observe the rules of etiquette fundamental in Japan. Proving that you're not a barbarian will insure warm welcomes not only for you but also for other American travelers who follow in your footsteps. For instance:

Baths (o-furo): *Wash off first, then get in.* They are usually very hot. Do not reduce the temperature in a bath unless you are the last one in. If you can't bear it, tell the host "O-furo wa chotto atsu sugimasu" ("This tub is a little too hot") and perhaps they will tone it down for you. Reheat the water before you quit the room.

In places with a hot spring-fed tub (known as "onzen") you may not be able to get in unless your temperature tolerance level far exceeds that of a Maine lobster. If it's a large bath, you may not do anything about it at all if someone is already in it. In small, spring fed tubs the temperature will recoup automatically, so it may be okay to cool it down a little at first. Make it bearable, but not so comfortable that you could stay in for a long time. If someone else comes along, they'll want it plenty hot.

Slippers: Wearing slippers indoors keeps the tatami mats on the floor clean. Shoes that have been worn outside *must not* be worn past the entranceway. The same applies to the wooden slippers provided for you to wear outside. There are separate slippers for the bathroom, too. In some nice clean places these are more a formality than a necessity, but in others the reason for them will quickly become apparent. Don't wear them out of the bathroom. Don't enter any room with tatami mats on the floor wearing any shoes or slippers unless they're provided at the doorway. The foremost concern of many ryokan and minshuku managers is whether foreign guests can be relied upon to observe their civilized customs, particularly those regarding footwear. (Speaking of feet, never clip toenails or fingernails in public; if you do so in private carefully dispose of the clippings, which the Japanese find unutterably disgusting.)

Tipping: In ryokan a small gratuity to the maid is customary. Don't hand over cash, though; this is considered very rude. Wrap your gift in paper, even facial tissue if nothing better is at hand. Tipping is not necessary in minshuku. If someone is particularly nice to you, buy them a box of candy at a store to show your appreciation, and have it wrapped.

Breakfast: By asking ahead of time you can nearly always get toast and coffee for breakfast if you'd prefer not to start the day with cold salted fish and rice with a seaweed relish. You may learn to love the Japanese breakfast—at least parts of it such as the rice or miso shiro soup—but few foreigners are crazy about raw egg for breakfast. In their beer, maybe, but in the morning...?

No Smoking Areas: The Shinkansen have them, as do larger ferry boats (ask for a "kinnen-sha" when you get your tickets). Elsewhere... bring your respirator. Though attitudes are changing and some Japanese people are cutting down or at least switching to milder brands, overwhelming numbers of the Japanese are still very much committed to their tobacco habits. Many jokingly refer to smoking as their hobby!

Japan Rail Pass

You'll need one of these. Public transport is the only sensible way to go in Japan. Driving, with some few exceptions, is too difficult and expensive.

A rail pass will save you a lot of money and time fooling around at ticket windows. There are two types of passes, besides child fares. "Ordinary" is a reserved seat in coach class. These are fine seats, but they can be a bit cramped for large Gaijin frames. If you can swing the extra cost (about $6 per day), I recommend a "Green Car Pass." Green Car seats are much more comfortable, your fellow passengers are much more reserved and their children are quieter. You'll arrive at your destination ready to do something other than search for peace and quiet.

A 21-day Ordinary Pass is 55,000 yen or $340; the Green Car Pass is 78,000 yen or $475. The passes are good on Bullet Trains, Expresses and ferry boats as well as buses and other transportation run by Japan Railways (JR).

You must buy an exchange order for your Japan Rail Pass before you leave the U.S. Your travel agent will be able to arrange one for you. If not, give him or her the phone number of the nearest U.S. office of Japan National Tourist Bureau (which can also sell you a rail pass exchange order). Their U.S. phone numbers are listed in the back of this book.

Activating Your Rail Pass: After clearing customs upon your arrival at Narita Airport, take your rail pass exchange order to the JTB office at the airport and receive the actual pass. A cab to downtown would cost around 12,000 yen or $75. If you intend to stay longer than 21 days in Japan, you're better off taking a regular bus into town and waiting to activate your pass until you're really ready to hit the old Tokkaido Road (Japanese for "dusty trail") out of Tokyo on Day 4. You can activate it then at the JTB travel agency by the main doors adjacent to the ticket office at Tokyo Station; allow an extra half hour.

Subways
In Tokyo, the Subway is the way to get around. Avoid the early morning and late afternoon rushes—mid-day is frantic enough. If you just have to see how tightly packed humans can get, go down to Ueno Station at 7:30 a.m.!

Getting around central Tokyo is easy enough, as most station signs are written in English as well as Japanese. Buying the correct ticket is the first challenge. One way to get the right ticket is to go to the Fare Adjustment window (midori-no madoguchi), say the name of your destination and hand over what you're sure must be enough money (maybe 300 yen; remember, these people are totally honest). Another, perhaps easier, way is to buy the cheapest ticket, then go to the Fare Adjustment window when you reach your destination and pay the balance due. Try asking passers-by how much to wherever you're going; you may get lucky and find an English speaker.

The next challenge is to get on the right train, and then get off at the right station. The following method works beautifully: simply smile and walk up to a likely-looking native holding your ticket and body in a questioning attitude. Say the name of your destination slowly and carefully. If they answer in Japanese and you can't understand, shrug and say "Gaijin-des" (pron: guy-jean-des: "I'm a foreigner"). The least you'll get is pointed in the right direction, and often you'll be led by the hand to the right track. The most likely people to ask for directions are 13- to 18-year-old schoolgirls. You may only get giggles, but there's a good chance you'll have a "would like to practice English" guide on your hands.

By the time you've used the Tokyo subways a bit, the rest of this trip will seem easy. Acting friendly and lost will get you an amazing amount of help. Often, particularly in rural areas, just the lost questioning posture will prompt some citizen to try and help you out.

Taxis
Taxis are temptingly easy to use. Once in a while, they're great; using them all the time will eat a huge hole in your budget. Take a taxi if you need to get somewhere in a hurry, if you're too tired

to deal with the subway, or if you're desperate for an air-conditioned ride around town. Also it's quite possible you'll be out late one night after the other public transportation systems have shut down (11 or 12 p.m. in most cities).

A red light in the window indicates that the cab is free (green light means it's occupied or reserved). Some places, such as train stations, have taxi stands—you must get in line and wait your turn. Elsewhere, just wave one down on the street. Hold your hand up with your palm flat. If you hold up one finger, it means you're willing to pay the flat rate. Two fingers out means you'll pay double. In extreme emergencies hold out three fingers—but at this rate, believe me it's *much* cheaper to wait a while longer. The more polite, clean and respectable you look, the easier it will be to get a cab.

Taxi rates go up 20% after 11 p.m., and there is a time charge in slow traffic.

When boarding a taxi, never try to open your own door. The left rear door is opened and closed mechanically by the driver. Don't do it yourself or you'll mess up all the little levers and doodahs the driver uses. Don't worry, he'll let you out when it's safe to do so. Exit only on the left side. Tipping is not necessary, and I don't unless a driver has been especially helpful or waited around a lot at no charge.

Buses

Traveling by bus is less fun than other transportation modes, but it's sometimes the only way to get to the more secluded areas (hitchhiking excluded). Luggage is difficult to handle on buses, so try and get on board early and stow your stuff in the back of the bus.

The fares are usually posted on a revolving schedule at the front of the bus. Often, if you get on at the train station that will be square one on the fare system and you'll pay the highest fare on the list. Be sure to have correct change at hand when you get off so that you don't keep everyone waiting. On most buses you drop your coins onto a little conveyor belt gizmo as you get off; there may be a bill-changer next to the belt, but there usually isn't.

Boats and Ferries

Ferry and boat terminals are set up similarly to all other public transport in the country. You will normally have no trouble figuring out how to get where you're going. Many boat lines are privately run and your JR pass won't work. Don't worry—most are quite reasonably priced.

Car Rental

You will only rent cars twice on this suggested itinerary (Karatsu and Sado), and if you prefer not to drive you can get by with buses instead.

Renting a car is easy. You must have an International Drivers License (get one for a couple of dollars at any U.S. AAA office) and a major credit card. Cars can be rented with cash only, but the rent-a-car man will feel better if you show him a credit card. Cars can be rented on an hourly basis, so if you should decide at any point that you need a car for a morning, go ahead and get one. The most easy-to-find agency is Eki Rent-A-Car, with offices in front of most major and many minor train stations.

Driving: If you're slow and careful, you will have no trouble driving in the places I have suggested you rent a car—country and small town areas where the traffic is usually light. My advice is, don't rent in the larger cities. To a Gaijin it looks like sheer vehicular mayhem out on the streets of Tokyo. (In actuality, the Japanese drive far more skillfully than we do because the traffic moves faster on unbelievably narrow lanes that don't even have shoulders.)

The Japanese drive on the left. Take it slow and think where you're going to turn and which lane to turn into. Be particularly careful when you enter a traffic-free street. It's easy to get going the wrong way. The biggest danger comes when you're not paying close attention and you look up to see a car coming at you on what seems to be the wrong side of the road. The natural tendency is to jerk the wheel the wrong way. . .watch it.

The other main difficulty is navigating when you can't read the street signs. Again, this is not too bad in the country but very scary in big cities. Try to commit a roadmap to memory, and if possible have a passenger navigate for you.

Do not drink and drive in Japan. They are serious as a heart attack about that offense! Keep your speed down, drive carefully, use common sense and you should have no problems.

Money

The unit of currency in Japan is the yen. During the '80s the American dollar has fluctuated between 250 and 150 yen. Today $1.00 US is approximately 150 yen. To mentally convert prices from yen into dollars, drop the last two zeroes and subtract one-third. (750 yen = about US $5; 3,000 yen = about US $20; 15,000 yen = about US $100.)

Many places don't accept credit cards. Small restaurants and inns in the country seldom accept them. Still, a credit card will sometimes smooth your way. The American Express Card lets you get cash advances at their service banks in major Japanese cities. Visa and Mastercard are more widely accepted in Japan,

Basic Travel Methods

and you can often get cash advances on these too. A credit card will also make car rental easier.

Travelers checks are widely accepted in Japan. Use them as a safe vehicle for your money (about the only thieves in Japan I'm ashamed to say, are foreigners), but not for purchases. Exchange them for yen at a bank and pay cash whenever possible to minimize service charges.

Change money at banks—their exchange rate will usually be slightly better than at hotels. Most banks in cities and larger towns have a foreign exchange window or desk; transactions are handled efficiently and quickly.

Vouchers and meal tickets are quite common. For example, when you make reservations at the Minshuku Center, you will receive vouchers for ryokan, minshuku and rental car. You'll exchange them instead of paying cash, and nothing else is needed.

Similarly, in many restaurants—notably soba ya or noodle shops—you pay for your meal first and receive a ticket. Recognize these by noticing if the cashier has a large box of plastic or wooden tokens that he or she is giving out, or if people are buying tickets at a machine before approaching the counter.

ITINERARY

DAY 1 After a 13-hour daytime flight, you'll arrive in Tokyo at almost the same time of day as you left the U.S.

DAY 2 Confirm your travel arrangements for the trip, then see some of Tokyo's sights, Stop for lunch at a wonderful little noodle shop, and explore your new country.

DAY 3 This is a day to rest, recoup travel worn resources and see more of Tokyo. Save some energy for the Kabuki-za theater and the glittering Ginza this evening.

DAY 4 Leaving Tokyo, travel by Bullet Train to the Izu Peninsula, then train and bus through beautiful coastal scenery on the way to historic Shimoda. Spend your first night in a traditional Japanese minshuku in Toi.

DAY 5 Near your lodgings, view the coastal sights including Mt. Fuji, the seascapes of Matsuzaki and the gorgeous orchids at Dogashima as well as the pesky monkeys at Hagachi. Rest and really get over the jet-lag. Do only as you please. Maybe the beach is where you belong today.

DAY 6 Today you'll see how well Japan's travel network really works—ten boat, taxi, train and bus rides in six hours. Long but fun, with enthralling views. The views of the Izu Penninsula coastline, the Atsumi Penninsula and the Mikawa bay are breathtakingly scenic. Meet some country folks who don't see Gaijin every day. Practice your phrasebook Japanese.

DAY 7 Visit Japan's greatest national shrines. The Geku and the Naiku at Ise are the seat of Shintoism, Japan's own religion. Their grand, pure Japanese architecture will give you a real feeling for the ancient culture of Japan. Evening will find you in everyone's favorite Japanese city, Kyoto.

DAY 8 Explore the temples, shrines, labyrinthine alleys and shops on the eastern hillsides of Kyoto. Your feet will be all the transportation you'll need this morning. See the imposing Nijo Castle in the afternoon and visit the very Japanese Gion district for evening fun.

DAY 9 Take a side trip to Nara today to round out your education in classical Japanese architecture and history. Nara's temples are among the finest in the country and rank with the Shrines at Ise in cultural importance. So much to see and do that the day will be gone before you know it.

Itinerary

DAY 10 Today you're off to Shikoku, smallest of the main islands, and perhaps the least known to foreigners. Stop along the way at Himeji city to see the Shirasagi-jo castle, a feudal masterpiece. Continue across the Inland Sea to Shikoku and the small town of Kotohira. Climb the longest staircase you've ever seen (you'll love it) and see the Kompira Shrine, sacred to Japanese mariners.

DAY 11 Travel the length of Shikoku on a comfortable train and cruise through the finest neck of the Inland Sea on an even nicer boat to the gorgeous island of Miyajima. The evening will be free to stroll around one of the three most beautiful islands in Japan.

DAY 12 Feel free to relax and enjoy this splendid little island any way you please. Early morning might find you nearly alone watching the sun paint the famous red Torii in front of your ryokan. Walk all or part of the island's circumference. Have a tea lunch in Momijidani, the maple valley.

DAY 13 After a morning at the somber and sobering Peace Park in Hiroshima, buy a lunch in a small bakery to eat while the Bullet Train whisks you south to the the island of Kyushu. Arriving at Karatsu, rent a car for a drive out the peninsula to Hatomisaki and Yobuko town.

DAY 14 Drive around the peninsula and explore tiny narrow bays and inlets, with jewel-like villages nestled down in narrow canyon bottoms. Today is casual. Visit the rural morning market in Yobuko. If you want to sleep late, go ahead and sleep. The day is yours.

DAY 15 Back to the big city of Kyoto. By now you'll probably feel at home in your lodgings here, so you'll have no trouble entertaining yourself. There's a lot of Kyoto you haven't even been near yet, so wander around unfettered and discover your own favorite corner of this captivating city.

DAY 16 Travel by train to the western coast, a region of intriguingly different scenery and friendly people. Enjoy a low-key, high-class corner of the land. The Gardens at Kanazawa are among the finest anywhere.

DAY 17 Today is a long travel day. Again, the sights enroute more than make up for your pains. You will see the west coast of Japan out the window of an excellent train while enjoying regional specialties packed in keepable containers for lunch. From Niigata to the island of Sado you'll be lulled by the sound of the Sea of Japan.

DAY 18 Explore Sado as you drive yourself around an island so exotic looking you'll think you've been transported into an ancient oriental landscape painting. Pass one breathtaking view and charming coastal town after the other on your way to friendly little Negai.

DAY 19 Return by Boeing Jet-Foil to Niigata, then climb into the breathtaking mountains of central Honshu aboard an old (but comfortable) deisel train. You'll pass village after village to which you'd love to return.

DAY 20 Nearing the end of the trip, you'll see one of the most colorful shrines in all Japan. Admire the shrines of Nikko and the natural beauty of the lake and mountains around nearby Chuzenji. Wind up your day with a quiet evening "at home" in your ryokan, minshuku or pension, or a stroll around the romantic waters of the clear cold lake.

DAY 21 Today brings a bumper crop of sights. Ride the bus back down the hill to Nikko's Toshogu Shrine. A riot of color and intricate architecture awaits you here along with the original "Hear No Evil, See No Evil, Speak No Evil" monkeys. Nikko will make you feel like you're getting back on the beaten path, but you'll be a changed person—a traveler of Japan.

DAY 22 Time to complete the loop. A two-hour ride will return you to the place where you began nearly three weeks ago. Revisit old haunts or explore a part of the city you missed the first time through. Rest up for tomorrow's flight back to the United States. You won't forget this trip. I promise!

Sightseeing Highlights:
In this balanced 22-day tour of Japan you'll visit:

Castles and Palaces:
Imperial Palace, Tokyo
Nijo Castle, Kyoto
Castle of the White Heron, Himeji

Museums:
Metropolitan Art Gallery, Ueno, Tokyo
Bridgestone Museum, Tokyo
Tranportation Museum, Tokyo

Hall of National Treasures, Nara
Treasury, Miyajima

Natural Beauty:
Izu Peninsula
Dogashima Orchid Center, Matsuzaki
Hagachi Island (wild monkeys)
Ryoanji, Kyoto
Miyajima Island—Momijidana and Mt. Misen
Omishima Jinja, Yobuko
Undersea Observatory, Hatomizaki
Agano River and Bandai Uplands
Goshiki-numa (Five-Colored Swamp), Urabandai
Mt. Nantai, Chuzenji
Lake Chuzenji
Kegon no Taki Waterfall, Chuzenji
Sado Island

Parks:
Meiji Park, Tokyo
Ueno Park, Tokyo
Peace Park, Hiroshima
Kenroku-en Gardens, Kanazawa

Shrines (Shinto):
Meiji Shrine, Tokyo
Naiku and Geku Shrines, Ise
Kasuga Shrine, Nara
Kompira-Jijna Shrine, Kotohira
Itsukushima Shrine, Miyajima
Keta Taisha Shrine, Kanazawa
Futaarasan Shrine, Nikko
Toshuga Shrine, Nikko

Shopping:
Akihabara Electronics District, Tokyo
The Ginza, Tokyo
Tsukiji Fish Market, Tokyo
Sannen Zaka, Kyoto
Asa-ichi (Morning Market), Yobuku

Temples (Buddhist):
Asakusa-Kannon Temple, Tokyo
Hofukuji Temple, Shimoda
Temple of the 47 Ronin, Tokyo
Shuzenji and Shigetsuden Temples, Shuzenji
Kiyomizu Terra, Kyoto

Chion-in, Kyoto
Kofukuji Temple, Nara
Todaiji Temple (Great Buddha), Nara
Horyu-ji, Nara
Chuzenji Temple, Chuzenji
Myojoji Temple, Kanazawa
Rinnoji Temple, Nikko

Other Sightseeing Highlights:
Kabuki-Za Theater, Tokyo
Tokyo Tower
Harajuku District, Tokyo
Biragaso Mingekan House, Matsuzaki
Shuzenji-onzen Hot Spring Resort, Matsuzaki
Pearl Island
Gion Quarter, Kyoto
Torii at Miyajima
Aikawa Gold Mine, Sado Island

I hope you enjoy the tour and find this book as helpful as I intended. If you detect glaring errors or just want to communicate your thoughts on the tour, please feel free to write me care of: **John Muir Publications, P.O. Box 613, Santa Fe, New Mexico 87504**.

Happy Trails!

Day 1

DAY 1
DEPART USA—TOKYO

You've never seen a day as long as this one. You'll cross the international date line at 600 mph and arrive, after 13 hours in flight, at almost the same time you left. It will remain light for over twenty hours. Changing time zones upsets your circadian rhythms, resulting in jet-lag. Be sensible and the trip won't take all the wind out of your sails.

■ Rest well the night before your departure.

■ Carry a toothbrush and a fresh shirt to avoid that "air cargo" feeling on arrival.

■ Wear loose, comfortable clothing and shoes on the flight. Carry a light, warm sweater or jacket.

■ Sleep as much as possible on the plane. If you see an empty row in the middle of the plane, occupy it immediately. Four seats to sleep on beat first class for comfort. There's nothing to see out the window but water.

■ Carry a Walkman with language tapes, music or a book on tape. Thirteen hours on a commercial jetliner can seem like weeks.

ARRIVE IN TOKYO

Suggested Schedule

Arrive at Narita Airport.
Two hour bus ride to downtown.
Check into your hotel.
Muster your strength and get out on the town for a while.

Customs will seldom open your bags and you'll soon be out on the street. Trade your dollars for yen at one of the several bank-operated currency exchanges in the airport lobby. Travelers' Information Center (TIC), also in the lobby, can provide you with free maps, transportation schedules and hotel information. Be sure to get a map of Tokyo, Tokyo Walking Tour brochures and any other literature that looks useful.

Although you're probably tired after the long daylight flight, you still have a two-hour bus ride ahead. Airport Limousine buses will leave you at the Tokyo City Air Terminal downtown, with easy access to the subway system. Airport Express buses will take you to major hotels in the downtown area, including the New Otani. Both limousine and express buses leave frequently from in front of the arrival lounge.

The cheapest way to get downtown is the Keisei Skyliner Train, leaving from Keisei Airport Station.

If you want to activate your JR rail pass now, you can also take a JR train downtown. Take the shuttle bus to nearby Narita Station where the train will take you to Tokyo Station. If you intend to stay in Japan more than 22 days, then you should pay for the ride into town and save your pass for real traveling.

When you arrive downtown, take the subway or a cab to your lodgings. If it's anywhere near rush hour, avoid riding the subway with luggage.

Orientation

Tokyo is truly vast. The only quick way in and out of town is the Bullet Train, and even that takes time. Entire guidebooks are written about Tokyo alone.

Get out the map of Tokyo you picked up at the airport TIC and have a look at the general layout of the city. Tokyo is made up of wards and neighborhoods; the Ginza, Asakusa, Ueno, Akasaka, Shinjuku and Akihabara are the most interesting to first-time visitors. Each has its own distinctive character. Kasumigaseki is the commercial district. Akihabara is where you'll find electronic products. The Ginza has expensive shopping and entertainment. Roppongi is where Gaijin and young Japanese go to cavort. Shinjuku offers brilliantly lit, commercial, fun and sometimes seedy nightlife. Tsukiji is for fish, food and cookware shopping. Akasaka's nightlife quarter, fun for all, defies categorization. Ueno and Asakusa are loaded with shopping, museums, a zoo, temples and more.

Even more than New York or London, Tokyo would take several lifetimes to really get to know. Like painting the Golden Gate Bridge, by the time you got to the end you'd find that the beginning needed sorting out again. It is hectic and crowded beyond belief; but it is also safe, fun, energetic in the extreme and constantly changing. Learn it a bit and you'll love it.

Lodging

Tokyo has literally thousands of places to stay, ranging in price from cheap to absurd. Small interesting places are scarce and usually expensive. Ryokan, common elsewhere, are rare in the city. The rule is large western style hotels, of which there are many in all price ranges. The larger and more famous places such as the Okura, the New Otani and the Takanawa Prince are elegant to varying degrees and commensurately expensive.

The New Otani: Central location, vast facilities and a good members discount. Ask your travel agent (stateside) to inquire about a New Otani Club membership for you. It gives you a 10% cost break and entitles you to free breakfasts in a choice of restaurants with great views of the city and the fabulous New Otani Gardens. The membership takes a couple of weeks to process, so apply well in advance. There is a New Otani in Los Angeles (Ph# 213-629-1200) that can furnish details. The New Otani has a good place to leave luggage if you decide to take a side trip, good subway coverage with both Yotsuya and Akasaka Mitsuke stations in easy walking distance, and the greatest health club in the world for guests' use. Avoid room service and laundry and you'll be able to sleep two for around 18,000 yen $150 including complimentary breakfast.

Many small hotels are available in the 13,000 yen double oc- $110 cupancy range. Primarily for businessmen, they are usually not much to look at and lack character. One of the best is the **Hokke Club**, quietly located near Ueno's Zoo and Museums. Ph# 834-4131.

TaiEiKan Ryokan, In the Hongo area of Ueno near Tokyo $90 University, is traditional Japanese style inside and out. The service is personable and the breakfast is raw. At 5500 yen per person with breakfast the price is very reasonable for Tokyo. Ph# (03) 811-6226.

A homestay in a private family household near Tokyo is an inexpensive option if you have extra time. Asano-san and his helpers at the Minshuku Center can arrange it for you. A homestay is the best way to get "inside" the Japanese culture. Homestays are usually arranged for one week duration, but overnights are available too. The cost for one week with a family is around 25,000 yen for a couple—a very good deal. Only outgoing, seriously interested persons should apply.

These are a small sampling of the many places to stay in Tokyo. If you would rather be in a specific area such as Akasaka, ask TIC or a JTB travel agent, or have your agent at home help you with arrangements.

Food
Eating in Tokyo is simple; just follow your nose. As you walk the streets you will see hundreds of interesting little places. The variety would easily fill a tome twice this size. Be adventurous. Stick your nose into doors. Be ready for all kinds of responses from a glad welcome to a solid stony silence at the appearance of a bizarre apparition (you). Many places advertise their wares with plastic repli-food in the window. Don't hesitate to drag the waiter or proprietor out into the street as you point at your selection.

Tokyo has so many places foreigners haven't found yet that with enough exploring you could write your own book. When you return to the states, drop me a line about your discoveries.

Good Tokyo Restaurants, by Rick Kennedy, is a great guide to eating and drinking in this town. The book is widely available in Japan, or order it from Kinokuniya Books in Los Angeles, (213) 687-4447.

A famous and delicious place for tonkatsu or pork cutlet is **San Kin**, on the corner west of the Yotsuya station. Reasonable, very good and filling.

Want sushi? Wander around Roppongi and find your own little place. There are a couple of good ones down the hill behind the Almond Cafe at the Roppongi Kossuten.

For a good late night dinner or snack I love the **Inakaya** in Roppongi. It's a $30-a-person kind of place, but is it ever good and fun. This country style inn, very popular with the Gaijin in town, sets everything in front of you, cooked to order. Try the asparagus, the potatoes and whatever else looks good. A cedar box full of sake called masuzake is a good way to get your meal rolling. It's across from the defense agency (Bo-e-cho) one block northwest of the Almond on the south side of Gaien-Higashi Dori.

If Indian food sounds good to you, try the **Taj** in Akasaka. Take the subway (chikatetsu) to Akasaka-Mitsuke Station. Come out from underground, head southeast on the main drag, Sotobori-dori, half a block and you're there. It's across the street from the Akasaka Tokyu Hotel, in case you still haven't found it.

Go back behind the Taj to find the Akasaka night life zone. A place called the **Tiger Bar**, affiliated with the U.S. Hungry Tiger restaurants, is on the second street in to the west, about three blocks south of the station. Their happy hour, from 4:30 to 6:30, can't be beat for price or beer quality. Appetizers are pricey.

Nightlife

You name it, they've got it. How much do you want to spend? Got a couple thousand (dollars!) for the evening's diversion? Go down to the Ginza and have a ball. If you're a little poorer, don't worry. There are still a few thousand places you can go; you can't go wrong. Pick your area for the kind of fun you want. The really happening places change from week to week, but a few are landmarks:

In Roppongi, find the **Lexington Queen**, **Giza** or **Tsubaki Ball**. They are all in a one block area one block east of the Almond and south. Down at the south end of the quarter behind the Porsche dealer is a trendy new spot called **Cleo's**. Other hot places in the Roppongi area are **Masquerade** and **Les Choux**, down the hill towards Meguro.

Many Akasaka night clubs hang on forever. The names and

locations remain the same while their clientele, decor and entertainment evolve. I recently revisited an old haunt called **Byblos** up the street from the Tiger Bar. Interesting. Young. . .

Have fun wandering the streets, talking to people both local and foreign, and just letting go. You can't get hurt in this town—except from alcohol poisoning or an extreme case of "you've got to be kidding" when the bill comes. Seriously: Tokyo nightlife runs on affluent businessmen's expense accounts. A scotch and water can cost from US $7 to $50 depending on the neighborhood.

Have fun!

Helpful Hints

Always plan to be doing something other than moving around during the morning and evening rush hours. Large subway stations such as Ueno and Tokyo turn into madhouses at those times.

Keep a map handy of whatever area you're in.

T.I.C. (Tourist Information Center) can give you helpful information, maps and a wonderful service called Japan Travel Phone (call the operator and say "Collect call TIC")—English-speaking consultants for any problem or circumstance that might befall you in the city or the boondocks. Teletourist, a taped 24 hour information service, is (03)-503-2911. Tokyo's main TIC office is at Kotani Bldg., 1-6-6 Yurakucho, Chiyoda-ku, tel. (03)-502-1461.

DAY 2
EXPLORE TOKYO

Your only "must-do" today is to confirm your travel arrangements. The rest of the day is free to see some of the sights at your leisure, visit a wonderful little noodle shop and explore a bit of Tokyo. Don't worry that you aren't seeing all the sights Tokyo has to offer. You'll get your fill of shrines and temples later on.

Suggested Schedule

	Early morning stroll around the neighborhood.
8:00	Breakfast in your hotel.
9:30	Visit Minshuku Center to pick up your reservations and coupons.
11:00	A stroll around Tenno Heka, the Imperial Palace, or the Bridgestone Museum.
13:00	Lunch at Yabu Soba.
14:00	Visit Akihabara.
16:00	Meiji Park for a restful stroll through "real" Japan. Possibly walk through Harajuku on your way out of the park. If necessary, return to travel agency.
Evening	Early dinner and bed.

Getting to the Minshuku Center
Take the subways to the Yurakucho Station. Immediately east of the station, in the first basement of the Kotsu Kaikan Bldg., you will find the **Tokyo Minshuku Center**, where you can make your lodging reservations for the trip (or pick them up if you wrote ahead).

Sightseeing Highlights

▲▲▲ **Meiji Shrine/Park:** Built after the Emperor Meiji's death to honor the man who opened Japan to the world, this park is a haven of tranquility—beautiful Shinto architecture and a peaceful environment in which to enjoy it. The large torii (gates) and the Iris Garden are particularly noteworthy. Try to be at the Kiyomasa Ido spring around closing time to sip crystal-pure water in a quiet, woodsy glade.

▲ **The Imperial Palace:** The Emperor's residence is not a major tourist experience. I'm sure that within are beautiful gardens, etc., but much like the Oval Office not just anyone gets

> **I cannot live without books.**

—*Thomas Jefferson*

University Book Store

SEATTLE:
4326 University Way N.E. • 634-3400
Mon.-Sat. 8:45-5:30; Thurs. nights 'til 9
BELLEVUE:
990 102nd Avenue N.E. • 646-3300
Mon.-Fri. 10-9; Sat. 10-6; Sun. 11-6

Day 3 37

DAY 3
MORE OF TOKYO

This is a day to rest, recoup faded bodily resources and see some more of Tokyo. You don't have to do everything on the suggested schedule. Go to the places that interest you or just go until you've had enough. Don't knock yourself out. Save some energy for the Kabuki-za theater this evening.

Suggested Schedule

6:30	Tsukiji Fish Market.
8:00	Breakfast in your hotel.
9:00	Tokyo Tower for a view of the city.
10:00	Sengakuji.
11:30	Tsukiji for lunch—sushi-sashimi or soba.
12:30	Ginza for windowshopping.
13:30	Bridgestone Museum.
Afternoon	Ueno Park or Asakusa Shrine.
Evening	Kabuki Theater and an evening out and about.

Sightseeing Highlights

▲▲▲ **Tsukiji:** If you're an early riser, go down to Tsukiji Fish Market at first light (or before) to see more fish than one can even imagine in the ocean—a daily haul to feed one of the world's largest population centers. Almost all of Tokyo's fish comes from this neighborhood. The action starts before daylight and is worth getting up early for. Join the fishmongers for an excellent and reasonably priced lunch (their dinner) in the neighborhood. Don't worry; it's immaculate and doesn't even smell of fish. You'll find the market just to the south of the Tsukiji stop on the Hibiya Line, in southeastern Tokyo.

▲ **Tokyo Tower:** If it's a clear day the Tower (a half-size replica of the Eiffel Tower) is worth a couple of hundred yen for the great panorama of the city it affords. Take your map up and familiarize yourself with the lay of the land. On a clear day you can see Mt. Fuji.

▲▲ **Sengakuji:** The Temple of the 47 Ronin, the 47 masterless samurai. Revered as examples of true loyalty, these men gave their lives for their master who was wrongly sentenced to commit seppuku (ritual suicide, vulgarly called "harakiri"). It's a beautiful little temple, shrouded in mystery and reverential silence. A copy of the story in English is available from the shops at the temple entrance. The book makes good reading on the train or in ryokan and minshuku late at night.

▲ **The Ginza:** Some of the world's most valuable real estate—
and the prices in the stores reflect it. You don't need to purchase anything, just have a lot of fun looking. Great toy stores
and depaato (department stores). Spot out the Kabuki-za
Theater, where you may return tonight for a show. Maybe purchase your tickets now.

▲▲ **Kabuki-za Theater**, Ginza: This famous theater offers the
fun spectacle of kabuki with a distinct advantage for foreign
tourists: English translations are available for a small charge.
Kabuki come in two varieties; jidaimono and sewamono.
Jidaimono is historical drama with great heroics and sacrifice in
the traditional Japanese manner. Sewamono is intimate drama
about common folk. In both types the main theme is conflict
between one's duty and what one would like to do. Full of wild
cross-eyed, swivel-necked theatrics, samisen music and clack-
ing hyoshigi sticks, it is a uniquely Japanese art form that one
should not miss. Admission ranges in price from 1500 to 10,000
yen and the English Earphone Guide costs an additional 600
yen. Daily matinee and evening performances.

▲▲ **The Bridgestone Museum:** Surely one of the best little
museums anywhere. Renoir, Cezanne, Matisse, Degas and
Picasso, as well as great Japanese artists, all in a little place you
can easily see in an hour. Open daily from 10:00 am, admission
800 yen.

▲ **Ueno:** Tokyo's "Central Park" contains a great zoo, with
what must be the most famous pandas in the world, along with
several museums and galleries. You could easily spend all day
here. Be sure to visit the zoo—great aviaries. If museums ring
your bell, you could spend another day in the Tokyo National
Museum and the Tokyo Metropolitan Art Gallery.

▲ **Asakusa-Kannon Temple:** A reconstruction of the original
destroyed in World War II. The Sensoji Temple temple was
begun by three 7th century fishermen who brought up a small
statue of the the Goddess of Mercy in their nets. Nakamise
street, the approach to the shrine, is typical of temple en-
tranceways throughout the country. Enjoy the shops for their
tradition and folk art. They're there to tempt the Japanese
pilgrim as well as the foreign tourist. You might want to buy a
good luck charm to ward off colds during your trip, or perhaps
prayer beads. An incense burner in front of the shrine spews
smoke that will cure what ails you. In front of the temples you'll
find a fountain of water with long-handled bamboo cups. Rinse
your hands and your mouth (spit the water out) in ritual cleans-
ing before entering the temple.

▲▲ **Tea Ceremony (Chano-yu):** The traditional tea ceremony
is an essential accomplishment for polite young Japanese
women and an incomparable cultural experience for foreign

Tokyo: Ueno

[Map showing: Tokyo Nat'l Museum, Tokyo Metropolitan Art Gallery, Zoo, Rinno-ji Temple, UENO KOEN, Nat'l Western Art Gallery, ASAKUSA, ASAKUSA KOEN, Sensoji Temple, UNIV. OF TOKYO, Ueno Eki, UENO, 5-Story Pagoda, Tachi Soba, Ueno no-mori Art Museum, HONGO, Shinobazu pond, NAKAMISE, Ochanomizu Eki, Electronics Shopping, AKIHABARA, Post Office, Akihabara Eki, Transportation Museum, Yabu Soba, SUMIDA-GAWA]

visitors. Several major Tokyo hotels, including the Imperial (504)-1111, the Okura (582-0111) and the New Otani (265-1111) feature afternoon demonstrations; reservations are required. Tea ceremony and flower arranging classes for foreign guests are held Thursdays and Fridays 11:00-15:00 at the Sakura-kai Tea Ceremony Center (951-9403) in Shinjuku.

Food

Tsukiji, just a short hop from Sengakuji, has the best soba or sushi you've ever tasted. Try **Maruyo Soba**, a little stall just south on Shinohashi-Dori from Tsukiji-kossuten, the main crossing. Fantastic soba! Kakiyage-soba is noodles, broth and mixed veggies. Kakiyage-ten-soba is the same, with tempura shrimp thrown in. "Shuniku kudasai" gets you more watercress in your kakeyage. If you want added ingredients, just point. Cheap. Or try **Takeno** restaurant. From the south corner of Tsukiji Honganji Temple turn left down Harumi-dori. Go down past the end of the temple. On the next block across the street you'll see several small alleys. Second from the southeast end is the one you want. Look for the phone number 541-8698 on the sign and you've got it. Great fish, cooked and raw, with or without rice, and excellent tempura.

In Ueno, You'll find a good stand-up noodle stall, **Tachi Soba**, under the train overpass to the right of Ueno station's north entrance. Very reasonable and the best broth anywhere.

Omote-sando: If you've got a craving for pizza made in Japan, go to the **Sabatini Pizzeria Romana**. Get off at the Gaienmae Eki stop of the Ginza Line and look for the big Suncrest building. In its basement is the pizzeria. Enjoy the food and the company—young Japanese, Italians and a scattering of Americans. 2000 yen gets you dinner with room left over for an ice cream across the street at **Haagen-Dazs**.

Ikebukuro: For sake in a cozy-funky atmosphere, my new-found favorite is **Sasashu**. Rick Kennedy's book and detailed maps showed me how to get there. Good luck. If you find it, you'll be glad you don't have to drive home.

DAY 4
IZU PENINSULA—SHIMODA—TOI

Today you'll leave the modern madness of Tokyo on a journey around the Izu Peninsula, whose sheer-cliff seascapes, varied terrain and tumultuous history combine to create a beautiful first experience of rural Japan. Along the way, stop to visit a temple dedicated to the first U.S. Ambassador's Japanese mistress, as well as an authentic Japanese country home. Tonight you'll stay in one of Japan's nicest minshuku.

Suggested Schedule	
8:21	Leave Tokyo Station (eki) for Atami.
9:15	Change at Atami for Ito and continue south for Shimoda via Izu Kyuko Rensha and bus.
10:45	Arrive Shimoda.
11:30	Taxi from Shimoda Eki to Biragasu Mingekan.
2:00	Bus from Shimoda to Matsuzaki and change to bus to Toi.
3:30	Arrive in Toi, check into your minshuku.

The Izu Peninsula
Izu is the Japan you came to see: ragged rocky coasts, surging seas, winding ways and friendly folks. The Izu Penninsula is much loved by the Japanese for it's natural majesty. Originally it was a place of exile for such notable Samurai as Minamoto Yoritomo and Sannetomo Minamoto. Their descendents are still here and their hokkori (pride) still abounds in the people of Izu today.

You are starting your journey in the same place that the original occidental (western) explorers did. Commodore Perry and the first U.S. Ambassador to Japan, Townsend Harris, lived in Shimoda during the mid 1800s.

William Adams, a ship's pilot, lived here in the 1600s and built the first western style ship in Japan for the Tokugawa Shogun at the village of Ito. *Voila*, the plot of the book and TV movie *Shogun*!

While in Shimoda and Toi, notice the Tudor-like cross-hatched Namako-kabe architectural style, peculiar to this area.

Transportation: Tokyo to Shimoda
Re-read the section on basic travel methods over breakfast and try and be out the door early enough to miss the 7:30 rush.

Tokyo to Toi

Take the subway to Tokyo Eki. You can activate your rail pass, if you haven't already, at the JTB office by the ticket office. The Bullet Train ticket window is in the middle of the station on the eastern side. It is a short ride to Atami; what you'll see out the window is mostly urban sprawl.

At Atami, get to the ticket window again. Your rail pass will take you as far as Ito, where you must buy a ticket for the local, private train down the coast.

At Ito, change again for Shimoda. It's the same line and direction but a local (futsu rensha).

Sightseeing Highlights—Shimoda

▲▲ **Hofukuji Temple**, near the station, is worth a visit. It is dedicated to Okichi Tojin, the mistress of Townsend Harris. She was ordered by the Shogun to look after Harris. In the ensuing years, she and Harris became lovers. Like sailors since time immemorial, his tour being up, he sailed back home to wife and family, leaving her with a broken heart and worse—much worse—the stigma of having been the first Japanese woman to fall for a gaijin. Tainted and trapped by the conflict of cultures, she took the only possible recourse. She swam out to sea to drown.

▲▲▲ **Biragaso Mingekan:** An old-fashioned country home, a rarity in Japan, it is un-touristy and entirely authentic, with a thatched roof, tatami floors, indoor hearths and antique furnishings. It is the home of Dacky Murakami, alias Patito, a Renaissance man who speaks fluent Spanish, English, French and probably others. Ask him what "ergonomy" is, and be sure and see his match-striker. For a small donation you're welcome to wander around to your heart's content. Don't get so wrapped up in his smoky little ante-room that you miss the other three floors of the house. A cab driver will find the place easily for you and it is a cheap ride from the station.

Transportation: Shimoda to Toi

After brief sightseeing and lunch, you'll find your bus from Shimoda to Matsuzaki at the train station. The buses can be crowded but the scenery along this route will more than reward you for your pains.

The town of Matsuzaki isn't much to look at, but it's rugged sea-sculpted beaches certainly are. Have a look before you make the short bus ride up to Toi (pron: "toy"). You may return here tomorrow.

At Matsuzaki, change buses to Toi. If you just say "Toi, kudasai," in a curious questioning manner you will have no trouble getting on the right bus.

Arriving in Toi you're only a short walk away from your lodgings. From the bus station turn right up the hill across the bridge and turn right again. Down the hill is a park along the beach. Go south to the end of the park and you will come to a row of buildings. The Shio Kaze is the third building down. Next door is the Mihama.

Lodging

Shio Kaze: Mrs. Suzuki, who runs this minshuku, is like a Mom if the house is not too crowded and you're a likeable sort. The excellent food and a room with a view of the waves lapping outside will leave no doubt that you're in the "real" Japan. If you can reserve a corner room ("kado no heya"), do so. Ph# 05589-8-0740. Rooms cost from 4000 to 7000 yen with meals.

Mihama So: If you can't get a room at the Shio Kaze, get Mrs. Suzuki to fix you up here, a five-second walk across the alley. The folks are very nice (the same family runs both places), the baths are large and the rooms clean. The ocean view is the same as at the Shio Kaze, and so are the prices.

Food and Nightlife

John Lennon, the only bar in town, is next door to the Mobil Station and upstairs. Kanezashi Yoshio-san owns both the gas station and the bar. Most evenings he can be found there amid the Beatle memorabilia. Though he speaks no English, he's a very friendly, helpful person. Show him your copy of *Japan in 22 Days*, please—he'll love it.

If you elect to eat out, there is a nice place up the main street about four doors from the gas stand. The sushi is excellent and the kushikatsu (pork cutlet and egg with rice) is divine.

DAY 5
TOI AND MATSUZAKI

View the sights, rest and really get over the jet-lag. Do only as you please. Maybe the beach is where you belong today. A short bus ride south will have you back in Matsuzaki, where you can walk and enjoy the extraordinary rock formations at your leisure. Further south by boat are the boisterous monkeys of Hagachi.

Suggested Schedule	
9:30	Walk the beach a bit and see the town.
11:00	Bus (or walk) down the coast to see the Dogashima Orchid Center and fantastic rock formations. Keep riding the bus on down the coast if you like.
13:00	From Matsuzaki, boat to Hagachi to see "wild" monkeys romping on the cliffs.
Afternoon	Continue your tour of the peninsula or return for a swim in Toi.
Evening	Rest and recreate. Have a long bath in the lovely o-furo in your minshuku.

ALTERNATIVE: Visit Shuzenji-onsen for the day.

Sightseeing Highlights
▲▲▲ **The scenery** of the coast. Matsuzaki, 2½ miles south of Toi, is well worth a visit, as are all the view points along the way. Bizarre rock formations. From many of the overlooks you can see Mt. Fuji as it is best seen: in the distance.

▲ **Dogashima Orchid Center:** Great orchids, what can I say? On the way to Matsuzaki.

▲ **Hagachi-zaki:** Wild monkeys and more beautiful coastline. Watch your handbags, ladies—the monkeys are wild, alright. A 45-minute boat ride from Matsuzaki.

▲▲ **Shuzenji-onsen:** One of Japan's most famous hot-spring resorts—overbuilt, overpriced, but a fine resort. The Shuzenji Temple merits a visit. The tombs of Minamoto Yoritomo, founder of the Kamakura Shogunate, and his brother are here. The Shigetsuden Temple across the river from the tombs is a serene little gem. Buses run frequently all day from Toi.

DAY 6
ISE

Today is an adventure in public transportation—ten boat, taxi, train and bus rides in six hours. Don't let the schedule intimidate you. It's more fun than a day at Disneyland. The views of the Izu Peninsula coastline, the bus trip out the Atsumi Peninsula and the ferry ride across the Mikawa-wan are breathtakingly scenic. This is also your first chance to meet some country folks that don't see Gaijin every day. Have a go at conversation.

Suggested Schedule	
8:00	Breakfast downstairs.
9:00	Walk over to the ferry boat pier, south of the hotel.
9:30	Blue and white ferry to Numazu.
9:45	Cab from boat terminal to Numazu Eki.
10:53	Local to Mishima for the Shinkansen.
11:28	Kodama Express to Toyohashi.
12:40	Run, don't walk, out the station and to the right for the Atsumi-sen train for Tahara.
12:45	Local train to Tahara.
13:20	Arrive Tahara and walk to bus stop, up the street to the light and to the left about 15 feet.
13:37	Local bus to Irako-zaki.
14:30	Arrive Ferry Terminal and get ticket for 15:15 ferry to Toba.
15:15	Welcome to Ise! Taxi to Toba Eki (walk NE if you are so inclined). First available train to Kashikoshima, call for boat to come take you across the lagoon to the Ishiyama So Minshuku.

Transportation

Today's first leg on the ferry to Numazu follows the sheer coast of Izu. Walk down the beach from the minshuku to the sea wall south of town and buy a ticket for Numazu on the blue, white and red striped boat at 9:30. You want the small passenger boat, not the car ferry. The price, 2200 yen per person, may seem a bit high, but the alternative is a 2000 yen bus ride that takes twice as long.

Take a cab for the short ride from the ferry terminal to the Numazu station. Use your rail pass for the local hop to Mishima

Day 6

Toi to Kashikoshima

where you catch the Shinkansen Kodama for Toyohashi. The Kodama Super Exress leaves Mishima at exactly 11:28.

Arriving in Toyohashi you have to move fast to make the local connection on the Atsumi-sen ("'sen" means "line"). Exit the station to your right and bear right along the station wall to another, smaller station immediately next door. If you hear the whistle blowing, forget the ticket; get on the train and buy your ticket from the conductor. This train is not covered on your JR pass—440 yen, please.

You'll arrive in Tahara at 13:20 with plenty of time to walk up the street to the stop light and make a left where the bus stop will be in front of you by the coke machines. The bakery on that corner also bears looking into.

The bus ride takes about an hour through rural Japan and offers tantalizing glimpses of the Atsumi Bay on your right. The cost is 800 yen.

At the ferry terminal you have time to get your 1000 yen ticket. Make yourself a snack or get some sóba at the stand inside. Notice the whale harpoon outside the terminal. (The last Japanese whaling expedition left for Antarctica in October of 1986, and Japan has agreed to stop killing great whales at the end of the 1987 season thanks to extreme international pressure.) The Ise-Wan Ferry ("'wan" means "bay") takes an hour. You should be on the 3:15 ship.

From the Toba Ferry Terminal, catch a cab again (no bus, at least not at the right time) to the Toba Eki. It's a 440 yen ride or a ten-minute walk. At the station go upstairs and buy a ticket for

Kashikoshima, just 25 minutes away on a gorgeous train. Before leaving, call the minshuku, Ishiyama So. Ishiyama-san will meet you at the station when you arrive.

When you arrive at Kashikoshima, go downstairs and walk straight down to the waterfront where the inn's small boat awaits to take you across to the minshuku.

Lodging
Ishiyama So: Kashikojima, Ago cho, Shima gun, Mie ken, Ph# 05995-2-1527. The people are nice, the accommodations clean and the view lovely. If you get the deluxe room for 8000 yen (with meals) you will have your own toilet and bath, quite a luxury in a minshuku. Other rooms are available for about 5500 yen. Meals are downstairs and the view is out front.

Daito: Same address, Ph# 05995-2-1136. Next door on the same islet is the Daito, much the same though the building itself has less character. Same prices, too.

DAY 7
ISE—KYOTO

Today you'll see Japan's greatest national shrines. The Geku and the Naiku at Ise are the seat of Shintoism, Japan's own religion. On the way, you can also shop at one of the world's largest cultured pearl centers, Mikimoto's Pearl Island. Evening will find you in everyone's favorite Japanese city, Kyoto.

Suggested Schedule	
7:30	Rise, eat and pack.
9:00	Leave for station.
9:30	Train for Ise-shi.
10:30	Bus from the #1 stop for Naiku.
Midday	Tour the Naiku.
13:00	Lunch at Sandoh (2nd floor 2nd block from Eki).
14:00	Walk to Geku.
16:46	Tokyu (express) train to Kyoto. #1 platform. Bus or cab to pension or ryokan.

Transportation
The Ishiyamas will boat you across the lagoon, and from there you retrace your steps of yesterday, passing Toba and going on to Ise-shi. If pearls interest you, see Mikimoto's Pearl Island—get off at Toba Eki and walk towards the ferry terminal—you can't miss it. Afterwards, simply catch the next available train to Ise-shi.

Ise Station has amply sized lockers in which to store your bags for the day. You can take a cab or bus to the Naiku (Inner Shrine). See the Naiku first, as you will then be in town after seeing the Geku. If you are busing it, the Naiku stop is to the right and in front of the station, just beneath the large cement torii (gate). It says number one, and it's the only one. The fare is about 350 yen. If there are more than two in your party, the cab will be as economical and quicker. After seeing the Naiku, return the way you came to the station or to the Geku.

After ranchi (lunch), walk up the street away from the station to the Geku, or Outer Shrine. See it at leisure.

The train connections to Kyoto are a little weak on this route so you have a whole afternoon before your leisurely ride to that city. Take your time at the shrines.

Arriving in Kyoto around 7:30, you are better off taking a cab to your nearby pension or ryokan. The cab will take you up the

Naiku

(Map showing: PARKING, MIKE-DEN, SHODEN, Koden-chi, TREASURIES, MAIN ENTRANCE, ANZAISHO, KAGURA-DEN, MAGATAKA, TSUCHINOMIYA SHRINE, KAZENOMIYA SHRINE, TAGONOMIYA SHRINE)

hill with your bags, whereas the bus won't. Tell the driver, "Shin Kiyo Mizu Miichi kudasai," and you will be taken to the right street. If you're staying at Kotomu, it is easily spotted on the dark street with its bright white sign out front. Teradaya is a hundred feet down the hill from Kotomu and to the left (north) in a little alley.

Sightseeing Highlights
▲ **Pearl Island:** In Toba, this is the home of cultured pearls. Frequent pearl-diving displays by the Amas (lady divers) make this place worth a visit. They usually bring up only edible seaweed but it is interesting nonetheless. Skip the long-winded explanation of pearl culture unless the subject absolutely fascinates you. Note: if you want to buy pearls, the little shop by the boat landing in Kashikoshima has much better prices than Pearl Island. Haggle, but not too hard.

▲▲▲ **Naiku:** The sanctum sanctorum of the Shinto animistic religion. Devoted to Amaterasu-Omikami, the Sun Goddess, it is built of hinoki (cypress) and the architecture is pure Japanese with no Buddhist influence. The buildings are taken down and reconstructed every twenty years at great expense (it has been done for possibly the last time since the necessary skills are dying out). The unusual architectural style with the gables and gold decoration is called shimmei-zukkuri. On your way into the shrine get a pamphlet from the police box in front of the entrance. If it is very crowded, my hint of the day is to concentrate on the Kazahinomi-no-Miya and the Aramatsuri-no-Miya shrines which are off to the sides. The tours focus only on the main, central shrine.

▲▲▲ **Geku:** The Geku, or Outer Shrine, is the residence of the Imperial family when they come to Ise. It is devoted to Toyouke-Omikami, the goddess of agriculture. The shrine is architecturally similar to the Naiku, with some subtle differences in construction. The hills around the shrine are nice to walk and relax in.

Geku

Map showing: Koden-chi, SHODEN, ARAMATSURI-NO-MIYA, MAIN SHRINE, TREASURY, MISHINE-NO-MIKURA (Rice Store), KAGURADEN, UJI BRIDGE, SAIKAN (Purification Hall), KAZAHINOMI-NO-MIYA, ISUZU-GAWA, PLACE OF PURIFICATION

Note: photography is discouraged at both the Geku and the Naiku. You will see Japanese people taking pictures, but if you use your camera, be discreet about it. Better yet, buy slides.

Food: Naiku
Sandhu: Lunch can be had quite reasonably and edibly in this working-man's place. It's on the second floor, on the second block up from the railway station towards the Geku (southeast). Spagetti Meato or Pizza Tosto are both decent. The lunch special is the Seto, working man's food. Say, "Ran-chi seto kudasai."

Pearl: A coffee shop with great coffee and o-shibori (hot or cold napkins depending on the season), near the station, if you have an hour to kill waiting for your train. Look for the Key Coffee sign out front, second block up from the station on the same side of the street as Sandhu.

Lodging: Kyoto
Pension Kotomu: Gojobashi, Higashiyama-ku, Kiyomizu shin-miichi, Kyoto. Ph# 075-531-1848. The location is lovely, quiet and very convenient. Ask for the top floor room (there are only two). It has a nice balcony with a view of the city and Kiyomizu-tera. After three days this will feel like your neighborhood. Staying at Kotomu you will be doing Kyoto as if you lived in a little apartment on the hillside, not a hotel room downtown. The boss, Hirae-san, will take very good care of you. The price is fair, too, for Kyoto. 5000 yen per person includes breakfast.

If you can't get into Kotomu go to **Ryokan Teradaya** 583 Higashi Roku-chome, Gojobashi, Higshiyama-ku, Kyoto. Ph# 075-561-3821. Just down the street a half a block from Kotomu, this inexpensive ryokan caters to foreigners and locals alike. Pleasant, but without the view Kotomu has. The price is excellent at 4000 yen with breakfast.

DAY 8
KYOTO

Wake up and walk 100 yards to the beautiful Kiyomizu Temple to begin your tour of Kyoto's eastern hillsides—winding shop-filled alleys where a temple or shrine will greet you at every corner. Kyoto, the imperial capital of Japan for a thousand years, is overflowing with history and traditional architecture.

Suggested Schedule	
9:00	Kiyomizu Tera.
Morning	Walk across the hillside via Yasaka, Shoren-in and Chion-in to the Heian Shrine and possibly Ginkakuji.
	Lunch.
Afternoon	Nijo-jo and whatever else you'd like to see.

Orientation
The Heart of Japan (Nihon no furusato) is how the Japanese think of this city. As the seat of government from 794 to 1868, its political fortunes waxed and waned but the essential spirit and culture remained, as did the Emperor. It is home to many of Japan's Buddhist sects, with over 2000 temples and shrines. Everywhere you look, buildings and gardens evoke a strong feeling of antiquity and culture.

The city was laid out along the lines of Xian, the ancient capital of China, in a grid plan that makes it easy to get around. You can nearly always see the mountains that ring the city on three sides, so it is easy to keep your bearings.

The Kamo River flows along the eastern side of the city where many of the principal sights are located. Follow the river and you can't go too far wrong.

There are temples everywhere so it is impossible to say where a tour should begin. It is best to see the city in sections and don't attempt to see it all. See what you can, at a meditative pace. Don't skip here to see there. It is all worthwhile and enjoyable.

Maps and advice in English can be had from the TIC, located up the street in front of Kyoto Eki in the base of Kyoto Tower, the space-age-looking beast visible from anywhere in town. While there, be sure and pick up copies of the Kyoto and Nara Walking Tour Courses. These are very handy little brochures.

The JTB office is outside and to the right of the central exit to Kyoto Eki.

Scan your Walking Tour Course pamphlet with a map of the city alongside to get the lay of the land. Maps can be had, along with a great selection of English-language books, from Maruzen Books on Shijo-dori.

When your hillside stroll is over, take a cab or bus to the other side of town for the walking tour of Kinkakuji and Ryoanji, or go and saunter around the grounds of Nijo-Jo. If your feet hurt too much for another walk, the Nijo castle is easier on them.

Trains, buses and the one-line subway are easy to use. The routes are marked on the city maps given out by the TIC.

Evening entertainment is found all over the city, ranging from the alleys of the Gion Quarter, lined with very expensive geisha houses, to the youthful, fun Kawaramachi district. The areas between Sanjo and Gojo-dori abound in fun and fascination. Wander at will, safe and sound.

Kyoto is nearly everyone's favorite city in Japan. See what you can and come back later for more.

Sightseeing Highlights

▲▲ **Kiyomizu Tera:** Built in 1633 by the Tokugawas, it is a National Treasure. The sanmon (entrance) is in classic Kyoto style. Past this entrance is a three-storied pagoda, then the hondo (main hall). The hondo's terrace, supported by 139 wooden pillars, affords a fine view of the city. In front of the hall are the sandals of the giant who was defeated by the dwarf Issunboshi. Past the terrace, the Otowa Falls are intended to be prayed under. Behind the hondo, be sure and see the Jishu Shrine. This colorful little shrine is devoted to Okininushi, the Japanese cupid. See if you can find the chief priest and speak to him. He is a Rotarian and a very gregarious fellow. The whole place is open during daylight hours. A fascinating sight is the monks, required by the order to beg for their food, working the neighborhood early in the morning for breakfast.

▲ **Sannen Zaka:** Down the hill from the main entrance to Kiyomizu a little alley rambles across the hillside. Sannen-zaka has some of the loveliest folkcrafts you'll see anywhere in Japan at very reasonable prices. It's on the way to Yasaka and the rest of the walking tour.

▲▲ **Kinkakuji:** At this writing, both Kinkakuji and Ginkakuji, the Silver and Gold Pavillions are closed to the public in a dispute with the city over the Historic City Preservation Tax, a local political dispute that unfortunately puts these major sights off limits. Check to see whether they've reopened by the time you arrive.

▲▲ **Ryoanji:** Ryoanji is quintessential Zen (whatever that may mean to you, Grasshopper). The fifteen rocks surrounded by white sand represent whatever you want them to—cloud

Kyoto

shrouded mountain tops or islands in the stream. It is the world's most famous rock garden.

▲ **Chion-in:** Home to the Jodo sect, it has a huge gate and Japan's largest bell. On your way across the hill, it is well worth a stop if only for the peace and quiet one may find here.

▲▲▲ **Nijo Jo:** Built by Tokugawa Ieyasu in 1603, this castle was the residence of several Shoguns (supreme military rulers of united Japan). Tokugawa Ieyasu built it, and it bears testimony to his style and daring. Within, the Ninomaru Palace houses paintings by Kano Tanyu. The whole place is impressive and elegant. Take your time. The gardens and buildings are as good as it gets in Kyoto, which is to say, in Japan. Closed on Mondays; admission is 450 yen.

✕ ▲ **Gion Corner:** A touristy but fun spot to get a look at the "classic arts," such as Gagaku (ancient court music), bunraku (classic puppet plays) and dancing by geisha and maiko (apprentice geisha). It is in the center of the Gion Quarter.

Food

Kyoto has its own food, known as Kyo-ryori or Kyoto cooking. Edo-ites (Tokyo folks) say that the southerners' food is too sweet and lacks salt or flavor. Perhaps true, but whatever it lacks in salt it makes up for with exquisite presentation and extraordinary delicacy. There are several types available: yusoku-ryori (concoctions for the Imperial court), shojin-ryori (Buddhist vegetarian food) and kaiseki-ryori (food prepared for the tea ceremony). All are available in many places of varying exclusivity. A commonly available version of kaiseki-ryori, the kyo-bento (a mouth-watering box lunch) is available in the basements of several large depaatos in town.

Kyoyamato Ryotei, right across the street from Ryozen Kannon has a very Japanese-looking gate and gravel path leading into a garden. This is a wonderful but expensive kaiseki-ryori place. If you don't think you can stand the price tag on lunch (5000 yen), at least have a look in the yard. If the old man is in the office in the entryway say, "Chotto misete ii deska?" ("'May I have a look?'") and he will say (you hope), "Hai, hai, hai, dozo" ("'Yes, yes, go ahead"). The view of the Yasaka Pagoda from here is the best in town and the gardens are so typical of Kyoto that you'll remember them forever. Perhaps plan to eat there on your third day in town. (Call ahead for reservations; someone from your pension or ryokan can call for you.)

A lunch option if you want to try kyo-ryo at a reasonable price (3000 yen) is **Mutsumi**, a lovely establishment, less fancy than Kyoyamato. The food is, all the same, very Kyoto. It is just in front of the east gate, the Torii of Yasuka Jinja. Reservations are a little less mandatory here but won't hurt (Ph# 525-0623).

Tohka Saikan: Chinese food. One of the few pre-WWII restaurants left in Kyoto, it is in a large building along the river on the west side of Shijo-dori bridge. The decor is like a set for an old Charlie Chan movie—pure Chinatown. Try their gyoza, fried pork dumplings, or the chien ti kua, tasty sugared fried sweet potatoes. The view over the river at night from the top floor dining room is excellent.

Torisei: Yakitori, neighborhood style. Go down Kiyomizuzaka (Kiyomizu's main entrance) to Higashioji-dori and turn north (right). It is in the middle of the second block up. All kinds of chicken. Everything you can do to chicken (except chicken and biscuits). Say to the chef, "Omakase shimasu" ("Please choose for me") and get a selection—all cooked, don't worry.

Nightlife

Make a point to see the Gion Quarter after dark. It will make you feel that you are in old Japan. If you're reading the book *The 47 Ronin*, you'll have a pretty good idea of what goes on behind those mysterious little doors. It is fun, but very expensive. If you can arrange for a Japanese businessman with an expense account to take you, fine. Otherwise, enjoy it from the outside.

The Kawaramachi area is more affordable. I've never been anywhere twice, in many nights of wandering this area, and I've always had fun. If you are unsure of what a place will cost, order a beer or cocktail and then ask for the check.

The Kiyamachi area is loaded with hostess clubs. Stay away unless you feel like being fleeced. If you're offered little hors d'oeuvres the second you sit down, beware.

DAY 9
KYOTO—NARA

A side trip to Nara today will round out your education in classical Japanese architecture and history. Nara, the original seat of government, today occupies a very important place in the nation's cultural conciousness, along with the Grand Shrine at Ise.

Suggested Schedule

8:52	JR line from Kyoto Eki to Nara. (You can save 26 minutes by taking the Kinki Nippon Line to Nara, but you have to buy a ticket.)
9:56	Arrive in Nara. See what you wish of Nara. Return when you like, even into the evening hours. Trains run every hour back to Kyoto, until 21:00.

Orientation
There is little left of the original Nara. Founded in 660 B.C., the city has suffered vast swings of fortune's pendulum. It was the original seat of government where Jimmu Tenno sat as the first ruler of ancient Yamato, the Land of Great Peace. During the period up to 784 A.D. the area was the cultural center of what is now Japan. Much was imported and assimilated from the T'ang Dynasty of China. This blending of Chinese and Japanese created the unique society and culture that lives on in 20th century Japan.

Nara has lost some of its charm to modern industrialization, but the past is still vivid in many corners of the city, from back streets to the beauty of outlying Tenri. And Nara still has the Daibutsu, an enormous Buddha statue you won't forget.

Sightseeing Highlights
▲▲ **Kofukuji:** The Temple of the Establishing of Happiness is the home of the Hosso Sect. It originally belonged to the Fujiwara family (9th-11th centuries). It was razed in 1180 after the fighting monks of the temple backed a loser in a civil war. Rebuilt, then burned again in 1717, it has been faithfully reconstructed. The central feature, Nara's trademark, is the five story pagoda. The Chu-Kondo (central main hall) is worth visiting but the Nan-en-do is usually crowded; you might skip it

if you can't get in the door. Nearby is the hall of Miroku Bosatsu, an image of the Buddha-to-be.

▲▲▲ **Kokuho-kan:** The Hall of National Treasures is filled with priceless relics from all over Nara, brought here to be preserved against pollution and fire—an unequalled treasure house.

▲▲▲ **Todaiji:** Great Eastern Temple, home of the Daibutsu, the Great Buddha. Founded in 745, it was to be the headquarters of all temples in Japan. It is the largest wooden building in the world, truly impressive. As you enter the Nandaimon, the great south gate, notice the Kongo-rikishi, lightning wielding devil gods. Inside you will come to the Daibutsu-den, the Hall of the Great Buddha. Huge pillars support a ceiling hidden in twilight.

The Daibutsu: Dainichi-Nyorai, the Great Sun Buddha, sits in all his imposing bulk in the gloom of the huge hall. All other Buddhas and Bodhisattvas are beneath him in the hierarchy of Buddhism. Originally cast around 750, he has been redone in pieces due to fire damage. He is 71 feet tall and weighs 551 tons.

▲ **Kaidan-in:** West of the Daibutsu-den, this pine-enclosed Ordainment Platform is usually an island of quiet in the maelstrom of tourists swarming over the whole area. Built by the Emperor Shomu for the Chinese priest who converted him to Buddhism.

✝ ▲▲ **Kasuga Shrine:** Founded in the early 700s by the Fujiwaras, it is noteworthy for its profusion of stone lanterns (some 3000 of them). It is strikingly constructed of hand hewn timbers in the Kasugazukuri style, painted in vermillion and white.

▲▲▲ **Horyu-ji:** The oldest intact temple complex in Japan, it is reached by JR train from Nara Eki to Koriyama and then a 20-minute bus ride to the temple precincts. A prime example of the architecture of the Asuka Period, the home of the Shotoku Sect is one of the prime bastions of Japanese art, with works spanning the length and breadth of their history. The temple's kondo or main hall is the oldest wooden building in the world. The oldest pagoda in Japan is also on the grounds. "Must-sees" are the Todaimon and the Yume-dono, the Hall of Dreams. An afternoon's worth of sightseeing.

▲▲▲ **Tenri:** A different sort of sect makes their home in the town of Tenri, on the main JR line out of Nara. They are the Tenri-kyo, a very outgoing sect. Somewhat neglected by mainstream tourists, they welcome visitors in a less commercial manner.

Itinerary Options

There is so much to see in the Nara Basin that one day won't begin to be enough time. You might consider making time to stay here another day.

Day 10 61

DAY 10
HIMEJI AND KOTOHIRA

Ride the Shinkansen to Himeji, where you'll have time to visit one of Japan's best-preserved feudal castles, the Castle of the White Heron. In the afternoon, cross the Inland Sea to the island of Shikoku. Spend the night in the small town of Kotohira, site of Kompira Shrine. Feeling energetic? Want to stretch your legs after the train ride? Climb all 2668 stairs to the Inner Shrine.

Suggested Schedule

8:15	After breakfast, check out and head for Kyoto Eki.
9:13	Shinkansen Hikari to Himeji.
10:09	Arrive in Himeji with two hours to see the Castle.
12:13	Shinkansen to Okayama.
12:47	Arrive Okayama with twenty minutes to make connection to JR Express to Uno.
13:46	Ferry from Uno to Takamatsu.
14:54	Arrive Takamatsu with a half hour to make the Ashizuri 7 to Kotohira.
Afternoon	Check into your hotel (ryokan). Afternoon free to see the Kompira Jinja.

Transportation: Kyoto to Himeji
It's a short Bullet ride to Himeji where you have a couple of hours to see the castle. Arriving there you will have no trouble finding the Himeji-jo Castle as you can see it from the station. It's less than a kilometer up the street. There are lockers for your bags in the lobby of the station. If they are full you may be able to leave your bags under a table in the main ticket office. Ask nicely. As you really don't have that much time here, I recommend that you take a cab for the short hop up the street to the castle. This way you will have time to see the castle thoroughly and still be able to stroll back to the station in time to catch your next ride.

Sightseeing Highlight—Himeji
Shirasagi-jo, Castle of the White Heron: Begun in 1333, it has been added onto by subsequent rulers. Toyotomi Hideyoshi based here during his conquest of the Chugoku area. The castle

reached its present size in 1624. Five stories tall, built of rock, mortar and massive wooden beams it is a sterling example of feudal architecture—arguably the best castle in Japan. Nearly all the others have been destroyed by fire and reconstructed in modern times using cement rather than the huge wooden beams that give this castle its ancient, imposing feel. If you go in for castles at all (what real romantic doesn't?) you'll love this one. Catch it on a weekday when the crowds thin a bit and pretend you're the Lord of the Donjon himself. After seeing the castle, you should have time to walk down the boulevard and perhaps pick up lunch for the train ride.

Food: Himeji

There's a **Kentucky Fried Chicken** at the end of the arcade, one street over on the north side of the main drag. Maybe you feel like something other than noodles and shrimp today (we all have our weak moments); the Colonel-san cooks tasty train food. Otherwise, lots of shops selling noodles, sushi and the like line the street leading to the castle in Himeji.

Transportation: Himeji to Kotohira

Leaving Himeji, get back on the Shinkansen and ride for a half hour to Okayama. There you get off the train and onto the express for Uno. A short ride will have you there, and all you have to do is walk off the train and go directly onto the ferry, which runs frequently. A half-hour cruise will have you on the smallest of the main islands, Shikoku.

When you arrive in Takamatsu, walk into the main train terminal and get on the Ashizuri Express for Kotohira. This is the last leg, I promise. You'll arrive in Kotohira at 16:16 with plenty of time to find your lodgings and still see the Shrine.

Sightseeing Highlight—Kotohira

Kompira-Jinja: Dedicated to Omononushi-no-mikoto, this delightful shrine was begun in the mid-1600s. Many sailors come here to pray for safe voyaging. The most noteworthy feature of this shrine is its profusion of stairs, some 2668 of them. Climb as many as you possibly can—the Inner Shrine at the end is a wonderful place set in a grove of cedar and camphor trees. The road leading to the shrine is all stairs and pilgrim souvenir shops. Some of them have neat stuff, such as a great carved wooden dragon—priced not to sell.

If you are not up to climbing all those stairs, despair not. There is a way out for the weak of knee. Litter bearers will carry you to the top in a little wicker contraption, for what I consider far too little money. There's a 180-pound weight limit.

Day 10 63

Kyoto to Kotohira

Lodging

Kompira Prince Hotel: at Kagawa-ken, Nakatado-gun, Kotohira-cho, Esai 709, Ph# 0877-73-3051. This is a businessmen's hotel, close enough to walk to the shrine, although a cab is not a bad idea. At 4500 yen a night with breakfast (eastern or western), it is quite reasonable. You'll have western beds and a bath in the room.

Other lodging possibilities are two ryokan on the main road to the shrine, priced accordingly. Both are fairly nice; the more expensive of the two, the Kotohira Kadan, is worth the extra money. **Kotohira Kadan**, Kagawa-ken, Nakatado-gun, Kotohira-cho 1241-5, Ph# 08777-5-3232: the service is prompt and courteous to extremes. It is very traditional, and caters to the more affluent pilgrims that come to the Jinja. Rooms from 10,000 yen up. The other ryokan is the **Kotohira Bizenya**, at Kagawa-ken, Nakatado-gun, Kotohira-cho 1241, Ph# 0877-75-3232. Rooms are 10,000 yen.

There is a youth hostel, the **Kotohira Seinen no Ie**, on the hill behind the Kotohira Grand Hotel for 1400 yen a night. It has a great location, the obasan (grandma) of the house is very nice, but it's none too clean. I once checked in and out in one hour. Maybe on a warmer night I'd have stayed: the view was very nice. Ph# 0877-73-3836.

Nightlife
Don't be out too late—you've got a lot more traveling ahead tomorrow. There isn't a lot to do in town after hours, anyway, but wander around and you'll find something.

An interesting drink to try here (or anywhere else, for that matter) is shochu lemon (pron: "sho-choo remon"), a potent concoction of rice liquor and sugared lime juice. An interesting place to try one is **The Rumi Bar**, just down the hill from the Grand Hotel. The establishment is rather expensive. You see. . .ahem, how shall I put this. . .there is company to be had. Sort of. It's a hostess bar, a charming provincial version of those hostess bars you should avoid in Tokyo and Kyoto. No real hanky-panky goes on. The girls will laugh at anything you say and maybe rub their knee against yours—but that's all. You're expected to buy them a beer or the like. The boss, a real gentleman, found me a room once when none were available in town. (Wives and girlfriends may or may not enjoy this place; mine finds it hilarious.)

DAY 11
MIYAJIMA

After traveling the length of northern Shikoku by train, board a high-speed boat to cruise across the most scenic neck of the Inland Sea, passing island after idyllic island en route to Hiroshima. Boat or train to the sacred island of Miyajima, where you'll spend the night.

Suggested Schedule	
8:12	Local from Kotohira to Tadotsu.
8:27	Express from Tadotsu to Imabari.
10:59	Arrive Imabari and cab (380 yen) to the Minato (ferry terminal).
	Lunch near the terminal, ticket (4100 yen) in hand.
12:35	Boat to Hiroshima through the Inland Sea.
14:38	Arrive Hiroshima and get a ticket for:
15:15	Boat to Miyajima (Utsukushima), 1080 yen.
15:35	Arrive Miyajima and walk to Ryokan.
Evening	Free to see the island.

Transportation
Be at the station early to get a seat—the local is crowded with school kids on their way to another day. Try talking to them; they all want to try their English on you, even if it's only "hello."

The ride is short, and you have only a short wait for your express to Imabari. The train is on the next platform over. Ask anyway, "Imabari wa nam ban desuka?" ("Which number [platform] for Imabari?"). If you can't count yet, have pen and paper in hand so they can write it for you. The scenery on the coastal sections of the rather long ride to Imabari is outstanding, and this is your main chance to see a chunk of Shikoku.

From Imabari Eki to the boat terminal is a short walk, but with luggage a cab is recommended. It's a base price fare ride and the base in the sticks is lower than in the city—380 yen. You have an hour and a half, so it's a good time to get lunch and maybe wander around the busy little port by the terminal. Get your ticket before lunch on the off chance that the boat might be full. On weekdays you'll have no problem.

The ride through the Inland Sea (Seto Naikai) is superbly scenic. The boat windows are washed daily, so viewing and photography are unimpeded.

Arriving in Hiroshima you have two options: the easy, more costly one or the cheaper, more difficult one. From the Ferry Terminal at Hiroshima, a boat direct to Miyajima leaves shortly after you arrive (1080 yen). For free (i.e., covered by your rail pass), you can take a train from near the terminal, through Hiroshima, to Miyajimaguchi where you can get a JR boat to Miyajima. The trip takes one and a half hours. I'd opt for more time on the island rather than on public transport. I don't want you to go broke; I just want you to see as much of the good stuff as possible.

Orientation
Miyajima, also known as Itsukushima, is ranked among the three most beautiful islands in the country. Until the reforms of the Meiji Period, no one was allowed to be born or to die on the island. Dogs were not allowed either. You're allowed to die there now if you want to, but you won't be buried there—and you still can't take your dog. To this day there is no cemetery on the island, and relatives of the dead must undergo rites of purification after funerals before they may return home. A favorite of the great founder priest Kobo-daishi, Miyajima is still revered today as a pure beautiful island.

Sightseeing Highlights
▲ The first sight that greets you upon arrival on Miyajima is a lineup of shops selling the usual snacks and souvenirs. The little automated bean cake making machines are interesting, even if the product they turn out isn't. Perhaps you'll like those sugary, beaney, brown confections, but I doubt it. Try just one before you buy a box.

▲▲ **Torii:** The great red gate out in the water (or in the mud, depending on the tide), one of the most photographed objects in Japan, is Japan's largest torii, 53 feet tall. It was erected in 1875 and is still in good shape today. Lovely at night.

▲▲ **Itsukushima Shrine:** Dedicated to the daughters of the Wind God, Susano. First built in 811, it has since been reconstructed many times. It is built in classic Shinto fashion with the many buildings separated by decking over the water. At high tide, the buildings appear to be floating on the water, as does the Torii, which is in line with the shrine. Dances are performed in the shrine for a fee, but the crowds make the viewing best from outside.

▲▲ **Treasury:** A modern fire and earthquake proof building, it is not much to look at, but within are 130 National Treasures.

▲ **Hall of a Thousand Mats:** Constructed in 1587 by Toyotomi Hideyoshi, one of medieval Japan's most powerful military leaders, and dedicated to his memory, the hall is said to

Day 11

Kotohira to Miyajima

have been built from the wood of a single camphor tree. There are really only about 450 mats, but it is impressive all the same.

Lodging

Ask the Tokyo Minshuku Center for help in finding reasonably priced accommodations on Miyajima. One possibility is **Kamefuku**, 849 Miyajimacho, Saeki-gun, Ph# (08294) 4-2111. 15,000 to 20,000 yen includes two meals.

If Miyajima is too expensive, or no lodging is to be found, stay the night in Hiroshima and commute to Miyajima for the day. It's less than an hour's travel each way, so this poses no great problem. Try exploring in the outskirts of Hiroshima—there's something to see in every small town between Miyajima and Hiroshima. Be adventurous.

DAY 12
MIYAJIMA

A day free to relax and enjoy this splendid little island. Miyajima, particularly on a weekday in fine weather, is an easy place to spend a day. See the main sights you missed yesterday. Ride the ropeway or better yet climb through Momijidani to the top of Mt. Misen. Or take an all-day hike around the island. Early morning and the evening are the best times to see the main sights unmolested by crowds. The day is yours to do as much or as little as you please.

Suggested Schedule

Forget about your itinerary. You're on vacation!

Sightseeing Highlights
▲▲▲ The view from the top of **Mt. Misen** commands a sweeping vista of the Seto Naikai. The Gumonji-do Temple at the top is a particularly fine viewing spot. Best in the evening when the crowds have thinned. The walk up from the bottom through the Momijidani or Maple Valley is breathtaking, particularly in the spring and fall. Tea houses in the valley make for a nice afternoon refreshment interlude. Just west of Momijidani is the ropeway to the top (800 yen). Why not ride it up, then walk back down?

▲▲▲ **Walk around the island.** An all day proposition, you can swim on seven lovely beaches and call it a pilgrimage. A picnic lunch (read "o-bento") from your ryokan or a restaurant is mandatory.

Itinerary Options
If you crave big city action, it's easy enough to go into Hiroshima for the afternoon and evening. Transportation is described in Day 13. You could see Peace Park and the Shukkeien Gardens today and sleep in tomorrow or head south earlier.

Miyajima Shrines

- TORII
- Ferry Terminal and Lodging
- HALL OF 1000 MATS
- DANCE STAGE
- PURIFICATION HALL
- DAIGAN-JI
- NO THEATER
- PAGODA
- ARCHIVE
- MARADO SHRINE
- ASAZAYA
- PAGODA
- TREASURY
- MAIN SHRINE
- Misen-yama, Momijidani
- SHRINES

0yd 25 50 75 100

DAY 13
HIROSHIMA—TRAVEL TO KYUSHU

Return to Hiroshima for a visit to Peace Park to see the place where nuclear war actually happened. Then head for Kyushu, the southernmost major island of Japan. The bullet train makes quick work of a long trip. Stay sober on the train—you'll be driving when you arrive.

Suggested Schedule	
8:00	Leave Miyajima via JR Ferry.
9:00	JR Local to Hiroshima Eki.
9:25	Morning free to see Peace Park and a little of Hiroshima.
12:25	Shinkansen Kodama for Hakata.
14:15	Arrive in Hakata and head for subway to Karatsu.
16:00	Arrive in Karatsu and rent a car.
	Drive to Yobuko or Hatomisaki, about an hour's leisurely trip.

Transportation: Miyajima to Hiroshima
Catch a ferry to the mainland around eight so as to make a connection to Hiroshima on the trains, which are crowded even though they run often early on. The JR ferry is in the first building in the ferry complex. Wave your rail pass at the ticket window and you'll know immediately if you have the right line. No ticket is necessary on JR locals—just your rail pass.

Once on the mainland at Miyajimaguchi, walk outside the ferry terminal and up the way to the west, across a rather large street to the big terminal. It's not the tiny station just outside the ferry terminal; that's a local that takes twice as long and costs real money. Go to the one that looks like a train station.

Ride the first available local to Hiroshima. The platform is across the tracks. Ask anyway. "Hiroshima wa nam ban desuka?" ("What number (platform) for Hiroshima?") The agent will probably respond, "Ni ban desu" ("Number two").

Arriving in Hiroshima about twenty-five minutes later, head for the lockers at the extreme south end of the station on east side. They are rather well hidden behind a coffee shop in the corner. Stow your gear and head for Peace Park (Heiwa Koen) by cab or bus. The cab is around 800 yen, the bus 200 yen. The bus stand is on the eastern side of the station.

Sightseeing Highlights
▲▲▲ Peace Park: At 8:15 A.M., August 6, 1945 an atom bomb was detonated on the civilian target of Hiroshima. The Chamber of Commerce stood at the epicenter. What is left of it is now called the Atom Dome. It and the rest of the park are very sobering indeed. The Peace Memorial Museum is full of grisly photographs and mementoes of the blast. Not fun, but something that everyone should see, including the leaders of a few countries I could mention.

The Monument to the Victims of the Atomic Bomb is an arch through which you can see the Atom Dome. On it is written, "Rest in peace, for this error shall not be repeated." This is very much the attitude of the people of Hiroshima. They don't want it to happen again—to anyone.

Transportation to Karatsu, then to Yobuko or Hatomizaki
Around eleven o'clock you need to head back to the station to catch a train for Hakata on the island of Kyushu. Before you leave, you might wander down into the underground shopping mall to get a bite to eat on the train. The bakeries down there that sell very good sandwiches.

If you can get on a Bullet to Hakata around noon, do so. If not, the 12:25 will do fine. Platform 11 for your train (check me—schedules change).

Ride the train for an hour and three quarters or until it doesn't go any further and you'll be at Hakata, Fukuoka City, the end of the line. Get off and head down to the well-marked subway. Buy a 200 yen ticket and get on a train for Karatsu. The 200 yen is for the inner-city underground portion of the trip; your rail pass covers the rest.

Ride until you reach Karatsu, again the end of the line. It will take another hour-and-three-quarters.

Had enough trains yet? If so, you'll be glad to rent a car in Karatsu. Otherwise, buses are also available to Yobuko and Hatomizaki. They are in front of the station, and there's an information booth in the station lobby.

If you are driving, take it easy at first. Read the section on driving in the front of this book before you take off in your hotrod. Keep to the coastal route and you can't go wrong. Getting out of town is the only hard part. If you pass a McDonald's, you're going the wrong way. Find out whether a Japanese "Biggu Makku" tastes the same as back home, have some great fries and be on your way in the opposite direction.

It's a half hour or so drive along the coast to Yobuko, a quaint little fishing town.

Hiroshima: Peace Park

*Map labels:*
- TOILETS
- ATOM DOME
- HON KAWA-GAWA
- MOTOYASU-GAWA
- MUSEUM
- PEACE BOULEVARD

1. STUDENTS' CENOTAPH
2. BELL TOWER
3. PEACE BELL
4. MEMORIAL TO UNKNOWN VICTIMS
5. KANNON STATUE
6. CHILDREN'S MEMORIAL
7. PEACE FLAME
8. MONUMENT TO VICTIMS OF THE ATOM BOMB
9. PRAYER SCULPTURE
10. AUDITORIUM
11. FLOWER CLOCK
12. FOUNTAIN
13. MEMORIAL HALL

Car Rental

Renting a car will make this a lovely wandering, exploring segment of your trip. I strongly recommend that you plan to have 19,000 yen set aside for this or a credit card you can worry about when you get home. Buses can take you where you're going, but it's fun to wander around this area and hard to get too lost. If you do decide to rent a car, Eki Rent-A-Car is just outside the station in a little booth in the parking lot. The fellows don't speak English, but if you show up with an International Drivers

Day 13

License (purchased from AAA at home), your regular license, preferably a credit card, and money in hand, you should have no trouble. Get a map and say "Yoboku wa doko desuka?" ("Where is Yoboku?"), and they'll draw a line for you. ("Map" is "cheezu" in Japanese, by the way. "Cheezu" also means "cheese" but that's irrelevant unless you really need a sandwich right now.) A two day rental for a car like a Toyota Tercel is 19,000 yen including insurance (hoken).

Lodging

Decide whether you want a real ryokan tonight. The price is a little bit higher, but the service is worth it and this might be a good place to splurge on a "real" Japanese inn. If expense is not a major concern, I suggest you stay one night at the Tsuruya Ryokan in Yobuko and one night at the Sea Side Pension on the cape. A more affordable option is to spend both nights at the Sea Side Pension. If the car rental cramps your budget, rather than forego it and take the bus, you could economize by staying at the National Citizens' Hotel in Hatomizaki.

Tsuruya Ryokan is in Yobuko, right on the water, and all rooms overlook the bay. You can toss rice crackers out the window to the fish. The service is much better than you usually get for the price, 8000 yen per person with two great meals. The place is a little on the old side but very nice. It is on a narrow little street on the opposite side of the bay from where you come into town on Highway 204. Keep going until you see a little bridge on your right, cross it, and bear right along the water. Go past a large grocery store and keep going down the lane. The ryokan has a little two-car parking lot on the opposite side of the street. Ph# 9558-2-3414

Sea Side Pension, Saga ken, Higashi Matsubara gun, Chinzei cho, Hado, 748-2 Ph# 09558-2-1288. A really nice psuedo-European pension for 6500 yen per person, beautifully sited on a hill overlooking the whole cape area—look for the new white building. Large amounts of western style food and beds (tatami, Japanese-style rooms are also available if you can't stand the thought of sleeping on a bed). Run by the Kubashima family. The views are great from most rooms.

The Hatomizaki **National Citizens' Hotel** (Kokuminsha) at Saga ken, Matsubara gun, Chinzei cho, Hado 1082, Ph# 09558-2-1511, is out on the cape. The location is lovely and the price is right, even if the place resembles a youth hostel (both private rooms and dormitory). The food is not so hot, and unless you're driving you're stuck here. I could think of worse places to be stuck, though. Around 3000 yen.

Itinerary Options

You are not seeing what most Gaijin see of Kyushu. The normal tour would include Nagasaki, a lovely city with a lot of Dutch influence, and at least one or two hot spring resorts such as Beppu or Ibusuki. If you have the time, any of these would make a pleasant two-day sidetrip.

Day 14 75

DAY 14
YOBUKO TOWN—HATOMIZAKI

Cruise the peninsula and explore. The coastline here is reminiscent of the fjords of Scandinavia—tiny narrow bays and inlets, with jewel-like villages nestled down in the bottoms. Today is casual. If you wake up early enough, see the morning market in Yobuko. If you feel you need to sleep late, go ahead and sleep. The day is yours.

Suggested Schedule	
Morning	Market or Asa iichi in Yobuko Town. See the fascinating boats and activity on the wharf. Drive to the Underwater Observatory Tower on Cape Hatomizaki.
Afternoon	Free to beachcomb or drive down the coast for a picnic.

Transportation
Driving, it's easy to get lost. Fortunately, you have ocean on one side and mountains on the other. Stick to the coastal areas and keep an eye on your compass. I don't read Kanji any better than you do, and I've never been lost for long around here. Most roads lead back to where you began, in Karatsu, less than an hour away.

Wander down along the coastline towards Hatomizaki and the Underwater Observatory. Bear right each time you have a choice of major roads and you'll find it.

Try some small roads and even a dirt road or two if you are so inclined. Explore with your wheels. A car gives you an unaccustomed freedom that you will soon love.

If you do get lost, as a last resort call the Travel Phone collect for help. Look in the back of this book for phone numbers, or just dial O and say "TIC collect call" ("Tee-aye-she, corecto-coru") in your best unaccented Japanese. Explain your situation to the person on the line, and they can translate to some helpful bystander you have managed to snag.

Sightseeing Highlights
▲ **Asa-ichi:** The Yobuko morning market is on the street just behind the main drag along the waterfront. Vegetables and the night's catch. It starts around 7:00 a.m. If you spent the night in Yobuko, you probably heard the boats going out at three in the morning.

Hatomizaki

▲▲ **Omishima Jinja:** My secret picnic spot in Kariya Wan. As you drive south, keep to the coast past the atomic power plant. Turn down promising roads until you come to a beautiful bay with a huge rounded rock formation and a little fishing village nearby. At the south end of town you'll find a small island surrounded by mud flats with a sea wall around it. Behind a large office building, a path leads up to Omishima Jinja, a wonderful, derelict little Shinto shrine. Over the hill is a sea wall with a back rest and a ship wreck to look at while you eat. (These directions are vague on purpose—after all, it's a secret. If you find it, please keep it clean. Thanks.)

▲▲ **Hatomizaki Undersea Observatory:** A tower lets you go down below the water level to view the thousands of fish that swarm along the coast. They chum the water, making for a spectacular number of little fish.

Food

As you leave Yobuko, there's a large grocery store on the south side of the road (away from the water), on the same street as the Tsuruya Ryokan. A good place to pick up picnic supplies, they have good bread, canned tuna and cute two-sandwich squeeze bottles of mayo, lemon, and cucumber. Sounds like a tuna fish sandoichi to me. They also have peanut butter and Japanese salamis.

DAY 15
HATOMIZAKI—KYOTO

Suggested Schedule	
8:30	Check out and hit the road to Karatsu.
10:12	Leave Karatsu by local for Hakata.
11:25	Arrive in Hakata and connect to:
12:02	Shinkansen for Kyoto.
16:33	Arrive at Kyoto Eki.
	Afternoon and evening on the loose in Kyoto again.

Transportation
Try and be on the road by 8:30 so you'll have a little buffer time in case of a wrong turn. A hint if you're driving—turn right out of the entrance road to the pension and the citizens' hotel. Head north on 204 toward Karatsu. Stay with the coast and the main road all the way to town. In Karatsu again, if you see McDonalds you have gone one street too far. Go around the block McD's is on, back one street, and make a left. You can see the station at the end of the street. Go past the parking lot where the car rental agency is and make a right. Cross the little bridge; to the left you'll see a gas station. Fill up and get the attendent to stamp the little white piece of paper the rent-a-car people gave you at the beginning. It should cost about 1600 yen if you drove quite a bit. Back at the rental stand, hand over the keys and the folder. You're done.

Board the 10:12 train for Hakata and ride it to the end of the line. You have a half hour there before your 12:02 departure. There's a bakery for sandoiichis but the food on this train is really tasty. ("What," you say, "edible train food?" Yes it's true. The food on this run, furnished by the Miyako Hotel Kyoto, measures up to their fine reputation.) I highly recommend the tonkatsu set, a heck of a good box lunch.

Ride that train all the way to Kyoto.

In Kyoto you have the late afternoon to check back into your hotel and stroll a bit before dinner. I leave the itinerary up to you. You're an old hand here now, right?

Day 16 79

DAY 16
TRAVEL TO HAKUI

Today you're off to the west coast—lovely to look at and, unlike the east coast, very sparsely populated. Agriculture, rather than industry, occupies most people here. In Kanazawa, stroll through one of Japan's most beautiful formal gardens. Overnight in the small town of Hakui, in a lovely traditional beachfront neighborhood.

Suggested Schedule

	Up early and be at Kyoto Eki for:
9:34	Kodama Express for Maibara.
9:55	Arrive in Maibara and change for:
10:23	Koetsu Tokyu for Kanazawa, Platform #7, but check anyway.
12:07	Arrive in Kanazawa.
	Free until three to see the Gardens.
15:03	Local JNR to Hakui.
	Cab to your minshuku. Remainder of the afternoon free for the sights.

Transportation: Kyoto to Kanzawa
It's a short ride to Maibara on the Kodama Express. Change there to a normal Express (Koetsu Tokyu) for Kanazawa.

Sightseeing Highlights—Kanazawa
▲▲ **Kenroku-en:** This is one of the three most beautiful gardens in Japan. It was created in sections meant to represent various aesthetic qualities: coolness, dignity, festivity, artistic form, spaciousness and scenic harmony. Laid out in 1837 for the Maeda family, it has everything a proper Japanese garden should have—grace, character, variety and tranquility.

A bus to the park leaves from the number 10 or 11 stop in front of the Kanazawa train station (150 yen for a short ride). You'll probably be happy for at least an hour and a half there but if you get tired you'll find enough to keep an inveterate shopper happy in the Korinbo and Kitamachi market areas, both near enough to the Station to make a quick cab ride feasible.

Food (Kanazawa)
At the station in Kanazawa they sell the best o-bentos you ever had. Kani-ben is a smoked salmon on rice, an ebi-ben is shrimp

and vegetables on seasoned rice and there are others. Take one on a picnic with you to the gardens.

Transportation: Kanzawa to Hakui
In Kanazawa, check the schedule for your last ride of the day, an hour on the local chugger to Hakui.

Upon arrival, take a cab to your minshuku, especially if you are staying at Tarosuke. It is a bit hard to find, but all the locals know the place.

Check in, then have a walk. If daylight allows walk down the beach to the cement torii, then turn up the hill to the shrine.

Hakui
The scenery isn't astonishing, and when you get to the station you may wonder why you are here. It really is a charming little town with a lovely set of shrines and temples. The people here don't see a lot of Gaijin, as most group tours head up to the better-known areas of the Noto Hanto such as Wajima and Nanao.

If it's warm out, the sea is right in front of the minshuku for swimming. Even if it's not, it's great for beachcombing. Never have you seen so many sand dollars.

Sightseeing Highlights—Hakui
▲▲ **Keta Taisha Shrine:** This small shrine has a sacred, virgin woods that the Emperor is very fond of. The Chief Priest, Mitsui-san is a famous calligrapher as well as a most agreeable and helpful gentleman. Search him out if you can and say hello. At the Shrine office you can get an English history of the shrine.
▲▲ **Myojoji Temple:** Down the road, a short bus ride from Keta Taisha or take the bus from the stop behind the minshuku. The temple belongs to the Niichiren Buddhist Sect, a relatively new group. About twenty years old, the five-story pagoda exemplifies new Buddhist architecture.

Lodging
Tarosuke: Located near the shrines in one of the nicest neighborhoods you will have the pleasure to see on this trip. Run by an obaa-san (grandmother) and her daughter. Obaa-san is a real sweetheart who will laugh with and at you. She is 80 years old, and I hope has lots more left to enjoy.
Ph# 1762-2-0616.

Food: Hakui
In Hakui you can eat in at the minshuku or walk out for a bite. If you're at Tarosuke, you have to walk a ways down the road to a restaurant near the freeway (east) to find anything. A place called **Mitakeya** has good reasonably priced food.

DAY 17
TRAVEL TO SADO ISLAND

Today is a long travel day. The sights enroute will more than make up for your pains. This scenery along this part of the west coast will impress you, the food in Niigata will tantalize your palate, and the Island of Sado will totally captivate you.

Suggested Schedule	
7:00	Breakfast. Get packed and paid up, leave your bags at minshuku.
8:00	Walk to Keta Shrine or bus to Myojoji.
10:15	Retrieve your luggage and be at station for:
10:37	Local to Kanazawa.
11:55	Hokuetsu Express for Niigata.
15:42	Arrive in Niigata, dinner, then cab or bus to the ferry terminal for:
18:50	Ferry to Ryotsu-shi on Sado Island.
21:20	Arrive (finally) on Sado. Bed probably sounds about right.

Transportation: Hakui to Niigata
Ask someone at the minshuku to call a cab to pick you up at 9:30. Say "Takushi kudasai, ku ji han goro." ("Could I have a cab around 9:30, please?") If you saw the Keta Taisha Shrine yesterday, but missed Myojoji, take a bus from the Taki bus stop behind the Minshuku to Myojoji. It is only a 3 km ride.

Back at Tarosuke, tell the cabbie, "Eki kudasai," to get back to the station. Catch the 10:37 local to Kanazawa. There will generally be no food on the train to Niigata until about halfway through the ride, when excellent o-bentos are brought on board. There are some shops in the basement of the Kanazawa station, and good o-bentos are available in the station itself.

From Kanazawa, ride to Niigata on the 11:55 express. The train ride north along the coast is scenic in the extreme: Snow-capped mountains of Chubu Sangaku National Park on the right and the Sea of Japan on the left. One could do worse for an afternoon train ride. Arriving at Niigata, get your tickets for the ferry boat. The **Sado Kiisen Agency** (travel agents), in a little booth outside in the front of the terminal, can take care of all your needs while on the island.

Food: Niigata
When you arrive in Niigata, you'll have a couple of hours on

your hands before your 18:50 ferry to Sado. I wouldn't call Niigata a really fantastic town to kill time in, but it has a couple of redeeming restaurants.

Jukoan is popular with the upward movers of Niigata. Run by a husband and wife team named Takegahara, this kushiyaki place will delight you with the range of flavors presented, many of them new to the western palate. It's not exactly cheap, but it is so good that you won't fret too much over two or three thousand yen apiece for a great meal. If the mistress is in, give her my regards and help her practice her English. You'll find Jukoan on Furuimachi-dori, a large shopping-mall street up the main drag from the station about 1½ kilometers. Bus up that way until you see a mall off on either side, then go north about two blocks. Jukoan, on the left, has a gray frosted glass door. Sit at the counter even if you have to wait a bit.

Your other option is to go to **Kotobukiya** for some fantastic Chinese food. Great gyoza (pork dumplings), delicious ramen soup—extremely piquant and filling, very reasonably priced. Kotobukiya is up the street from Jukoan in a little alley. Find Jukoan and ask for directions, both places are in the family.

Transportation: Niigata to Sado Island

After dinner in Niigata, take a bus to the ferry terminal. The bus depot is right in front of the station on the south side. The ride is short, but if you don't mind 800 yen the cab is easier after dinner. The ferry terminal is self-explanatory.

A pleasant (weather permitting) cruise will take you to Ryotsu City, where you will be met (if they're expecting you) by someone from the Sado Seaside. If not, take a cab to your lodgings, then to bed with you.

Lodging

Sado Seaside Hotel, 80, Sumiyoshi, Ryotsu shi, Niigata ken, Ph# 02592-7-7211, 4500 to 9000 yen. The hotel has a hotspring fed tub that you might enjoy if the day hasn't been altogether too long. The beach is nearby but you won't be needing it unless you are an early riser. In Aikawa a very nice ryokan is the **Yamaki Hotel** 361, Kabuse, Aikawa-machi, Sado-gun 952-15. More expensive (9000 yen) and also perhaps hard to find late at night. Or in Niigata, **Niigata Onoya Ryokan**, 981, Furuimachi-dori, Rokuban-cho, Niigata Shi 951.

DAY 18
SADO

Relax and drive yourself around an island so exotic looking, you'll think you've been transported into an ancient oriental landscape painting. You can't get lost—there's only one road.

Suggested Schedule	
Daytime	Sleep as late as you please (but not past nine) Pick up your rent-a-car and head out for: Aikawa—you should arrive around noon. See the mines. Continue around Sado until you reach the northern cape and the village of Negai. Check into the San Kei Kan.
Evening	Walk, swim and enjoy.

Transportation
First thing, get yourself organized with a car. Read the section on driving if you haven't already. A 24 hour rental period should cost from 9500 yen to 25,000 depending on how glorious a chariot you choose. The cheap model should be fine.

Head out of town for Aikawa. Get the rent-a-car man to put you on the right road towards Aikawa. Say "Aikawa wa dochira no ho desuka?" ("Which way is Aikawa?") and he should point out the direction at least. Go east over the biggest mountain you can find or across the narrow neck of the island and you should do fine.

Don't linger too long in the mines, because the drive north around the west coast is the main attraction today. You can't miss as there is only one road and one coastline.

Go north around the island until you get to what is obviously the northern cape, about a two hour drive if you don't hurry too much. This is Hajikizaki, the northern end of nowhere on Sado. Go around the cape until you see a resthouse/hostel on the right hand side of the road. Just past there about a half a kilometer on the left, a narrow road winds down the hill to the fishing village of Negai. The San Kei Kan Minshuku is the first in the line of inns on the beach.

Sightseeing Highlights

▲▲▲ **The scenery.** As you drive around the island, sheer, plunging cliffs, dive into the Sea of Japan. Offshore, tiny islets sport gnarled and twisted pines like ancient scroll paintings. Off to the sides of the main road, dirt roads and paths beckon to the adventurous. It's a wonderful drive.

▲▲ **Aikawa** is the sight of one of the oldest gold mines in the country. It's done up like an amusement park, but tasteful. The shafts are very interesting especially in light of the fact that they were built without machinery. The life size animated characters down in the hole would do Disney proud—very Pirates-of-the-Carribean-ish.

▲▲▲ **Crystalline waters.** If the weather is warm, you might consider getting a cheap dive mask from one of the shops in Negai. The water is gorgeous. The beach is rock but it makes for marvelous swimming all the same.

▲▲ **The path south from Negai.** Walking down the path from your lodgings you will come to grotesque rock formations and small shrines in tiny cliff-side grottoes. Fascinating.

Rent-a-car
In Ryotsu-shi, contact the Sado Kiisen (Agency for Sado Tourism), Ph# 02592-7-5195.

Lodging
San Kei Kan: Ryotsu shi, Negai 260, San Kei Kan, Ph# 02592-6-2440. The Kitazawa family runs this archetypal beach minshuku and a more hospitable group you won't meet anywhere. Ojii-san (grandpa) is the salt of the earth. It's worth learning Japanese just to speak with him. His grandson, Ryu-san, is a pal of mine. If you're lucky and he's not too busy with his school work, maybe he'll show you around a little bit. He is very bashful but toys and fireworks can help break the ice.

DAY 19
SADO TO BANDAI

Today you'll travel into the breathtaking mountains of central Honshu. The day starts with a drive down the stunning coast of eastern Sado, followed by a ride on one of the world's fastest boats, then a trip into the "Japanese Alps" on a rustic diesel train.

Suggested Schedule	
9:00	Leave Negai south to Ryotsu.
11:00	Jet-foil from Sado to Niigata.
12:00	Arrive in Niigata, bus or cab to Niigata Eki.
13:35	Local for Inawashiro.
17:39	Arrive in Inawashiro.
18:10	Bus to Bandai Kogen.

Transportation: Sado to Niigata
Allow an hour and a half for the drive down the coast to Ryotsu. When you drop the car off, the rent-a-car folks will take you back to the terminal for your jet-foil ride back to the mainland. Built by Boeing Aircraft, the jet-foil is one fast boat (50 mph).

In the row of shops behind the ferry terminal in Ryotsu-shi, you'll find beautiful Sado handicrafts—wickerwork and interesting curios—for sale at very reasonable prices, especially if you dicker.

Food: Niigata
McDonalds (in case you've weakened by now) is a three-minute walk from the terminal in Niigata. Walk two blocks west up the main drag and turn left. Keep an eye out for the bus terminal and the Isetan department store. By the way, Isetan runs the best department stores around.

Transportation: Niigata to Ura-bandai
When you arrive in Niigata, a bus will be waiting outside to take you to the train station. Get to the terminal and organize some lunch for the ride or eat here. The train to Inawashiro is a local all the way. The seats aren't the greatest, but the scenery is enough to keep your mind off your derriere and out the window.

You'll be winding up the Agano River most of the way to Aizu-Wakamatsu, passing through a dozen hot spring towns

Niigata to Chuzenji

that aren't even on the map. The people are friendly and interested to see foreign faces in this neck of the woods. You never know when you'll meet someone who has a relative in the States, or who has studied in L.A. Be outgoing and the people will respond to you. Bandai-Kogen (the Bandai Uplands) is loaded with quiet charm and armed with magnificent views of the imposing, steamy, volcanic Bandai mountains all around.

At Inawashiro, you have a short wait for a bus that takes you up the mountain to the resort village of Ura-bandai. Call ahead from the station to tell your pension that you're on your way, "Moshi moshi, [your last name] desu, ima Inawashiro eki ni imasu," and they'll pick you up at the bus stop.

Sightseeing Highlight
▲▲ **Goshiki-numa:** Five Colored Swamp is the unglamorous name of this gorgeous series of ponds formed by the eruption of Mt. Bandai in 1888. The waters run from aquamarine to blue to green and several other shades in between. There is a beautiful, spirit-lifting one-hour hike through pools, waterfalls and a profusion of trees. The trail begins (or ends) at Goshiki-numa Iriguchi and leaves you at the Bandai Kogen bus stop near the Pension.

Lodging
The **Ura-Bandai Pension Village** has some 30 pensions. All are nice. For information contact the Ura-Bandai Pension Assoc., Ura-Bandai, Fukushima-ken, 969-27, Ph# (02413)2-2004.

Pension Hozuki, Ph# 02413-2-2724, is lovely place nestled in the woods on a tiny lake. The beds are comfortable, and if the weather warrants it the floors are heated. Very nice for the price. The food is continental and well prepared. It would be nice to spend a week here during ski season. The hosts don't speak much English, but at this point in your trip you will manage fine anyway.

DAY 20
TRAVEL TO NIKKO

Nearing the end of the trip, you'll discover one of the most colorful shrines in all Japan. Admire the shrines of Nikko and the natural beauty of the lake and mountains around nearby Chuzenji. Finish with a quiet evening "at home" in your ryokan, minshuku or pension.

Suggested Schedule

7:30	Breakfast, pack and pay.
8:30	Walk the Goshiki Numa Trail.
10:15	Check out and get a ride to the bus stop.
10:45	Bus to Inawashiro Eki.
12:10	Local to Koriyama.
12:45	Arrive in Koriyama.
13:14	Leave Koriyama on Yamabiko #46 Shinkansen.
13:48	Arrive in Utsonomiya.
13:57	JR local to Nikko.
14:42	Arrive in Nikko.
	Catch the first bus up the hill to Chuzenji.

Transportation

After an early breakfast, walk or ask for a ride to the bus stop, where you can catch a bus for the short trip to Goshiki Numa Iriguchi. Perhaps your hosts will give you a lift if you ask. After a one-hour hike among the lakes you'll have plenty of time to get back to the pension and collect your bags, return to the bus station, and head for Inawashiro Eki.

From there it's a straightforward train ride to Nikko.

At Nikko, catch a bus to Chuzenji in front of the station. After the many tight turns of the famous Irohasaka Road, you will top out at the village of Chuzenji. 840 yen for the ride.

Sightseeing Highlights

▲▲ **Mt. Nantai,** an extinct volcano, looms over the magnificent setting of lakes and mountains. For an excellent view (if the weather is clear) ride the Chanokidaira Ropeway (600 yen).

▲▲ **Lake Chuzenji:** Cold, clear, sparkling beauty, unfortunately overcrowded most of the time. Admire it without the crowds in early morning or late evening.

▲▲ **Chuzenji Temple:** Chu-zen-ji means "middle zen temple." It is located around the lake to the left, just past the French

Chuzenji

[Map showing Chuzenji area with labels: CHUZENJI-KO, Nantai-yama, Minshuku Miharashi, FUTAARASAN CHUGUSHI SHRINE, Sanogoya Ryokan, Post Office, CHUZENJI TEMPLE, Kegon-no-taki, Chuzenji Pension, Lakeside Hotel, Chanokidaira Ropeway, IROHASAKA RD., IROHASAKA ROAD, To NIKKO]

Embassy's villa. You can usually get a lull between flag waving tours if you sit for a while and admire the lake. The tour of the main building and it's Tachiki-kannon, which doesn't take long, provides a great view and a good place to take pictures. Climb up inside the bell tower near the entrance—don't be bashful, get up there and give that thing a wallop!

▲▲ **Futaarasans' Chugushi Shrine:** A subdued yet elegant structure with some lovely cryptomeria trees and an enticing inner sanctum. As you stand in front of the shrine, the sanctum sanctorum is in the inner depths of a very long-looking hallway (the length is actually a rather good optical illusion to make you feel like a lowly mortal).

I had a chance to watch an elderly carpenter (daiku) re-work some of the old joinery of the shrine. He told me more and more religious structures (such as the Chuzenji temple) are being made of cement simply because there are no longer enough skilled joinery carpenters (moku-dai) who know how to make buildings like this one.

▲ **Kegon no Taki:** This waterfall is overrated, but since it is one of Chuzenji's best-known tourist sights (and right by the bus depot) you might as well take a look. The bottom viewing platform can only be reached by elevator (500 yen). Crowded.

Lodging
Sanogoya Ryokan, Tochigi ken, Nikko shi, Chugu shi, 2478 Ph# 0288-55-0091. When you arrive in Chuzenji, stay on the bus past the bus station at Kegon Falls and ride along the lake to the post office (yubin kyoku basu tei). If you get to Futaarasan Shrine on the edge of town you've gone one stop too far; walk back. Between the post office and a liquor store you'll find a cement path that leads up the hill. Walk up it and the ryokan is to the right. Tourist town prices prevail here—7500 yen a night. Sanogoya has one of the few authentic wooden o-furo I've seen in a long time. Good food and a nice view of the lake.

Chuzenji Pension, Nikko shi, Chuzenji Kohan, 321-16, Ph# 0288-55-0720. Popular among Gaijin, it has good food and private baths. Sudoo-san, the mistress of the house, speaks some English. Get off at the Kegon Taki Bus Station and walk south along the lakeshore a little less than a half a kilometer and you'll see it on the left. 8500 yen.

Minshuku Miharashi, Nikko shi, Chuzenji Kohan 2482, Ph# 0288-55-0103 (Makabe-san). A fine view of the lake, and reasonable comfort. The price is right—5000 yen. Walk past the pension another hundred yards or so toward Chuzenji Shrine and the minshiku is on the left.

DAY 21
CHUZENJI/NIKKO

Enjoy a slow-paced, pleasant day. Ride the bus back down the hill to the Toshogu stop and explore Nikko on foot. There are some good shops on the main road into town where you can buy a gift for the person who overwatered your plants and underfed your dog back home.

Suggested Schedule	
9:00	After breakfast, Catch a bus from the Kegon Station for the ride down the hill to Nikko.
Morning	See Toshogu Shrine and the Sacred Bridge.
Afternoon	Lunch in the neighborhood, see Rinnoji and whatever else you please in Nikko.
Evening	Rest and stroll around the lake.

Sightseeing Highlights—Nikko

▲ **Shinkyo (Sacred Bridge):** Originally reserved for the Emperor and his emissaries, this bridge is now used only on festival days. At this site the priest Shodo was said to have crossed the river on the backs of two huge snakes. The present bridge was built in 1902.

▲▲▲ **Toshogu Shrine:** Though some call it gaudy, most of us find this shrine's profusion of intricate decoration and bright color splendid to behold. Over 15,000 craftsmen were employed in its construction, completed in 1636. Outstanding features include the Five Story Pagoda at the entrance, and the Sanjinko (storehouse) whose unusual elephant carving was created by an artist who had never seen an elephant but relied on a literary description. The original "Hear No Evil, See No Evil and Speak No Evil" monkey carving is nearby on the lintel of the Stables for Sacred Horses. Further in is the shrine's centerpiece, the Yomei-mon (Sunlight Gate) with its lavish carving and adornment. Purchase your ticket for the whole shrine complex at Rinnoji Temple.

▲ **Rinnoji Temple:** A part of the main complex, this temple of the Tendai Sect was founded in 848 by the Buddhist saint Jikaku-daishi. It contains a profusion of statues dedicated to Amida-nyorai, the Thousand Headed Kannon and Bato-Kannon. Buy your ticket for the rest of the shrine here. 1500 yen gets you all the temples you can stand.

▲▲ **Futaarasan Shrine:** Founded in 767 (nearly a thousand years older than Toshogu), the shrine is devoted to the

Nikko Shrines

divinities of Mt. Nantai (formerly called Mt. Futaara). It is in three parts: The Honsha (main shrine), the Chugushi (middle shrine), and the Okumiya (inner shrine) on top of Mt. Nantai. For a fee you can walk up the mountain. It is a pretty stiff walk. Inquire at the temple's ticket window for prices. Visitors see the bright red Honden (main hall) and the inner garden with its holy spring and Bake-doro (goblin lantern).

Nightlife

There isn't any, unless you count the bar in the Lakeside Hotel (it used to have slot machines—now, alas, gone the way of the speckled-back mud dauber). Perhaps a flagon of sake would provide consolation? The liquor store by the Sanno Goya is well stocked.

Your best bet for the evening, after dinner at your lodgings, is a romantic moonlight walk along the lakeshore; or just sit and ponder the sights you've seen.

DAY 22
NIKKO—TOKYO

Back to the megalopolis! A two-hour ride will return you to the place where you began nearly three weeks ago. Revisit old haunts or explore a part of the city you missed the first time through. Rest up for tomorrow's flight back to the United States.

Suggested Schedule	
7:30	Have breakfast and get checked out.
8:20	Take the bus back down to Nikko.
10:05	JR train to Utsonomiya.
10:41	Arrive Utsonomiya and hurry for:
10:48	Shinkansen to Ueno.
11:34	Arrive in Ueno.
12:00	Lunch at Tachi Soba near Ueno station.
Afternoon	Check into your hotel, then do what you like with your last day. If you have money left, maybe go shopping in Harajuku, Shinjuku or Akihabara.

Return to Tokyo

This transportation segment needs no explanation to a Nippon vet like yourself.

As you return to your first lodgings, you'll feel that you've come full circle. Doesn't Tokyo seem different than it did the first time around? After a couple of weeks in country it should seem much less strange, more like a place you could get comfortable in. If you forgot to buy gifts for the folks back home, now's your last chance.

Shinjuku has several good discount camera/electronics/watch stores near the subway station. **Sakura Ya** and **Yodobashi Camera** are my favorites; haggle hard and buy several of one item to get the best deal. East down Shinjuku-dori you'll find a little of everything. The **Isetan Depaato** (department store) warrants a visit just to see one of Tokyo's (and the world's) best department stores. They sell bath salts from all the major hot springs in the country—unusual, good, inexpensive gifts.

Between Yotsuya and Shinjuku is a great shop, **Bingo-ya**. Done up like an old storehouse, it's full of authentically Japanese folk art and memorabilia, such as sandals of the type sold to pilgrims at shrines. Near the Dai-Ichii Hospital off Shinjuku-dori.

Day 22

Akihabara offers electronics galore. Great for household appliances, stereo equipment and toys. Wander and be amazed at how many shops there are. Go back into the little alley-like shopping malls where you can find everything from fuses to phone taps.

In Harajuku, shop **Kiddyland** for toys and the neighboring **Oriental Bazaar** for all those oriental nick-nacks people back home ask for, such as swords, kimonos and T-shirts. There are many other good shops in this district as well.

Return Home

Most U.S.-bound flights leave in the early evening from Narita Airport. Remember that two hour ride to the airport and leave yourself plenty of time. The easiest way to get out of town is to catch an Airport Express from the New Otani. Call there and ask the bell captain for details.

On the way home it will get dark right after take-off and stay dark for a very short while. You are racing back into the sun, going after that day you lost on the way over. Skip the in-flight movie and go to sleep if possible. Before you know it it's daylight again and time for a long day of customs, travel and homecoming. Returning home the jet lag is always worse for some reason. (This is a documented fact, not some personal delusion!) For the first few days you may find yourself falling asleep early, then waking up in the middle of the night with sleep nowhere in sight. It can be maddening, but don't worry—it will pass.

POST TOUR OPTION
HOKKAIDO

Hokkaido should be part of any tour to Japan. It wouldn't fit in the 22-day itinerary, though, without rushing you at a frantic pace through the rest of the country. Better to see some of Japan at your leisure, rather than more of it at a mad dash. Given an extra week you can enjoy Hokkaido too.

Before the mid-19th century, Hokkaido was a backwater inhabited by the aboriginal Ainu tribe and by outcasts from mainstream Japanese society. The vast mineral and natural resource wealth of Hokkaido changed all that when, in 1868, the Emperor invited economic development advisors from President Grant's administration. The rugged land and colder weather gave Hokkaido a character similar in many ways to America's western frontier.

Hokkaido's terrain is more alpine, and the people are inclined to be a bit rough and rustic. They are generally very outgoing and friendly as well.

Hokkaido doesn't have ancient temples or lore-shrouded shrines of the southern islands. Instead it offers a natural splendor altogether different from anywhere else in Japan. Its wide open spaces, spectacular vistas and many hot springs provide welcome relief from the bustling crowds of the southern islands.

Transportation

If you intend to see Hokkaido, get a one-week extension for your rail pass at the time of purchase for $170.00. Or an Excursion Pass (Shuyuken), available within Japan but not in Hokkaido itself, gives reduced rates for fixed-itinerary travel. The rate varies with your proposed route and length of stay but it does offer a fairly substantial savings. It must be purchased down south at major JR (Japan Railway) offices. Tokyo would be the obvious choice.

From Tokyo you can either fly to Sapporo in an hour for about $100.00, or ride the trains and ferry for fifteen hours. If you opt to fly, purchase a ticket at any JTB office. Flights north (as well as almost all domestic routes) leave from the old Haneda Airport. It's a half hour from downtown Tokyo by the monorail that leaves from Hamamatsucho Station on the Yamanote line. The trip north overland is interesting enough, though it does not rival the scenery you've already seen in other parts of Japan. Ideally you would fly one way and take the train the other way.

Post Tour Options 97

Hokkaido

Heading north, it is convenient to see some of the highlights on the way. Stops also help to break up the long trip. A sample itinerary for the ride north follows.

DAY 1: TOKYO TO HAKODATE

Suggested Schedule	
8:40	Leave Ueno Eki for Morioka on the Yamabiko Shinkansen.
11:25	Arrive in Morioka.
11:36	Depart Morioka on LEX Hatsukari, arriving in Aomori at 14:02.
14:50	Seikan Ferry to Hakodate. Arrive at 18:45.
19:02	Hokuto #9 to Sapporo. Arrive at 23:02.
Evening	Dinner in and early to bed.

Transportation
All connections are staightforward and well-marked on this major trunk route. The ferry connection is simple: get off the train and walk down a ramp to the boat. It is possible to get a night train to Sapporo if you can stand that much train riding.

The port town of Hakodate isn't a major tourist attraction—a hot spring resort and plenty of places to stay but nothing exceptional. The evening will be quiet.

Sightseeing Highlights: Hakodate
▲ **Asa-ichii:** The morning market, just down the street from the station, is full of produce, fish and crabs. Food stands on the sidewalk serve kegani (hairy crab)—the freshest, sweetest shellfish you'll ever eat. Great for a late breakfast.

A fellow here named Yoori is a self-taught linguist. He loves Spanish, English and Italian and will have a go at any others you might know and care to try him on. See if he speaks Swahili or Serbo-Croatian. Yoori's stand is right in the front center of the market. Look for a guy with a big smile and a white headband. He'll most likely grab you as you walk by.

The market is open every day but Sunday.

▲ **Mt. Hakodate Peninsula:** A short walk or cab ride (three kilometers or so) away, this penninsula has an interesting frontier waterfront flavor, your first taste of the difference between the northland and the south.

Lodging
Kita No Yado: In nearby Yunokawa Onsen, simple but decent minshuku accomodations. Nice hotspring baths, and washing machines which may come in handy. Ph# 0138-59-2092.

Akai Boshi: A small place where Chinese and German are spoken, a ten-minute walk from the station at 3-22, Asahi cho, Hakodate 040, Ph# 0138-26-4035.

DAY 2: HAKODATE/LAKE TOYA

Suggested Schedule	
8:00	Breakfast (or skip it and eat crabs at the morning market), walk along the beach.
9:00	Morning market, then see the peninsula.
11:38	LEX Otori for Toya.
13:36	Arrive in Toya, bus to Toyako Onzen.
Afternoon	Tour the splendid environs of Toya.

Transportation
The 2-hour train trip to Toya takes you through pond-speckled woods and along isolated wind-swept coastline. From Hakodate, get on the train that says "For Chitose," usually Platform #4.

In Toya, detrain at the main terminal. A bus will probably be waiting in front of the station to take you north along the lake to Toyako Onzen resort and your lodgings. The ticket is only 120 yen. It would probably be a good idea to get tomorrow's transportation sorted out today.

Sightseeing Highlights
▲▲ **Mt. Showa Shinzan:** This volcano sprouted in 1944-45 in a farmer's field, much to his surprise (he'd been expecting potatoes). It continued to grow for several months, peaking at 1,300 feet. Today it still steams enough to make you wonder whether it's really dormant. At the foot of the mountain is a museum commemorating the explosion with vivid displays. Nearby Mt. Usu (also reached by bus) has a multi-media show depicting the explosion. Another bus takes you to a ropeway you can ride to the summit for a good panorama of this lovely, mountainous country. The cost is 1000 yen. Just watching the fuming vaporoles from a distance is enough excitement for most people.

▲▲▲ **Lake Toya:** A round, deep, clear, gem of a lake with a cluster of islets at its center. For 600 yen you can take a ferry boat and stroll around the largest, Nakanoshima, as well as the smaller islets of Kannon, Manju and Benten. The temples there aren't fantastic, but the scenery is—especially in the fall. Buy cookies to feed the deer and save some for chumming fish from the pier. The ferry will leave you at each island for as long as you like, then you can catch the next one that comes by.

Lodging
Both places suggested below have volcanic hot-spring fed tubs on premises.

Ikoiso is a typical Hokkaido minshuku—good food, clean, but not much to look at. Ano-san, the proprietor, is a great cook. Put in your request ahead of time for a Toban dinner, an individual fondue-type dish of meat, vegetables and fish left to cook in their own juices until the flame beneath burns out or you just can't bear to leave it alone anymore. Superb. The lodge has a great location on the lake, away from the large tourist hotels, about two kilometers northwest of town. 5500 yen a night per person. The address is: Sobetsu-cho, Sobetsu Onzen, 83, Hokkaido, Ph# 01427552522.

Pension Ono has western-style beds and Japanese food for 6000 yen a night. Satoru-san, mistress of the house, is extremely pleasant and outgoing. 56-2 Sobetsu Onzen, Sobetsu-cho, Usugun, Hokkaido, Ph.# 01427-5-412.

DAY 3: TOYA-SAPPORO

Suggested Schedule	
	Rise when you please and break your fast, then bus into town in time to catch the 10:30 bus to Toya Eki.
11:38	Train to Sapporo (reserve ahead).
2:00	Check into your hotel.
2:30	See some of Sapporo.
6:30	Bathe and get ready for a night out on the town: Susukino and thereabouts.

Transportation
If Toyako-onzen seems crowded, reserve your return bus ticket to Toya the afternoon you arrive or first thing the next morning. You have a short wait in Toya for your train to to the big city, a 1½-hour ride through fairly interesting countryside.

Sapporo
This is a different kind of Japanese town. Laid out by American engineers and Japanese in western style, it is—believe it or not—square. You can find your way easily to anyplace on the map!

Pick up a copy of "Welcome to Sapporo" from the JTB office just down the street (Sapporo Dori) from the station. This is the easiest to use and most comprehensive map of Sapporo; it's also free. Sapporo Dori, the main north/south axis of the city, is intersected mid-town by Odori-park. The area bounded by the university to the north and Nakajima Park to the south is the center of attraction for out-of-towners, fun and delightfully easy to get around.

Sightseeing Highlights
▲ **The Old Clock Tower:** One block east of Sapporo Dori and three blocks south of the Sapporo Station, this is Sapporo's only surviving example of Russian Architecture. It was built in 1881 and now houses a library and an exhibit on the early days of Hokkaido.

▲▲ **Botanical Gardens:** Just west of the station, this park is jammed with all the flora and some of the fauna of Hokkaido. A great place for a picnic, with lovely walking trails through woods, meadows and swamplands. Also in the park are the Ainu Museum (presently closed) and, next door, the University Museum where for 100 yen you can see the rather bedraggled but unusual bird collection of British ornitholigist T.W. Blakiston. Admission to the park is 300 yen.

▲ **Pole Town and Aurora Town:** Two huge underground shopping arcades. Fun to wander around in, they epitomize underground life in Japan. Find them by descending into the subway in the uptown area. Shops and restaurants, including the ubiquitous McD's.

▲▲ **Maruyama-Koen:** 140 yen will get you a subway ticket from the uptown neighborhood to this park south of town. The southbound subway platform is down on the second sub level, just north of Pole Town. The signs are mostly in English, so finding it is no great task. Get off at Maruyama Koen station and walk west to the park. Once there, head for the elegant Hokkaido Shrine in the center of the park. It has the power and grace of the big shrines down south, but with heavy-weather durability.

▲ **Moiwa Ropeway:** You can get a cab from the Hokkaido Shrine to the ropeway. If the weather is good, the view from the top is grand. The full ticket, 1200 yen per adult, also lets you ride a little chairlift to enjoy "free" telescopes atop the viewing platform. If that seems a bit expensive, just buy the ropeway ticket for 800 yen and walk at the top.

▲ **Tannuki Koji Arcade:** This arcade, enclosed and above ground, has antique and miscellaneous shops at the west end. Gojyo Sakana Tsuuri-ya, the fishing shop on the second block from the west end, is famous in Japan. Mr. Gojyo is the man who makes $3000.00 fishing rods of bamboo and silk. He doesn't speak English, but if you say, "Aiyu tsuri no bideo o chotto misete kudasai" he may show you a video of this unusual kind of fishing and how his rods are made. Across the street is the most remarkably packed antique store you've ever seen.

Lodging
Nakamuraya Ryokan: Conveniently located one block east of the botanical gardens, this is a standard inn for Gaijin. Good food and friendly folks. Priced from 5500 yen up. Nishi 7, Chuo ku, Sapporo City 060-01, Ph.# 011-241-2111.

  Hotel Hokke Club: Ph.# 011-221-2141. 7000 yen per night.

  New Otani Sapporo: Fine rooms, excellent service—A very good hotel, well located in north central Sapporo near the station. If you are a New Otani Member from your stay in Tokyo, stay here. Ph.# 011-222-1111.

Food
Taj Majal Indian Restaurant: Between the Chisan Hotel and the Hotel Tokeidai. Mr. Raza, the manager, got me started in Sapporo with a great lunch, then found me a hotel when there were none to be found. Enjoy his excellent food.

Niijo-iichi-ba market: A bustling fish and produce market full of goodies from crab and smoked salmon to Sunkist lemons. (The three go exceptionally well together for a picnic in the park or in your hotel room. Hmmm . . . save some money and eat well.) Try the salmon jerky, too.

Sapporo Beer Garden: The order of the day here is Ghengis Khan (Gengisu Kan), named of course, after a famous Mongolian who apparently loved nothing better than to eat sheep and drink large quantities of beer. The old Sapporo Beer Brewery is the scene of Octoberfest-like drinking and eating. The waiter brings out large platters of meat, fish and vegetables which you then cook on a table barbecue. In the summer you can do all this outdoors for even more fun.

Nightlife
After dinner, walk into Susukino for nightlife. Susukino, by the way, is a type of marsh reed that flourished in the area before the locals decided they needed more nightclubs. More neon than anyplace this side of the Ginza, worth seeing at night even if you're not the slightest bit interested in drinking and carousing. If, on the other hand, you *are* interested, you've definitely come to the right place.

Noteworthy clubs in this area are **Club Exxing** and **The Maharaja**. I prefer Exxing, which advertises (for some reason) "Neurotic Romance." Big dance floor, great lighting. Admission (4000 yen) includes enough coupons to get yourself thoroughly filled with the liquid of your choice, plus food from a decent sushi bar. The Maharaja enjoys a more lively clientele on some days, but the management is not nearly as outgoing and flamboyant as at Exxing. It is, however, one of *the* nightclubs in Sapporo. Another club in the groove is the **Signife' Club**. Look for the sign under the neon Asahi Beer sign in the middle of Susukino. Each place costs around 4000 yen.

DAY 4: TENNINKYO

Suggested Schedule	
7:00	Check out and head for Sapporo Eki.
8:00	Train for Asahikawa.
9:30	Arrive and wait for the free bus to the Spa.
10:05	Bus to Tenninkyo.
11:00	Arrive at Tenninkyo and walk up the hill to your hotel.
	Note: Rail and Bus Timetables change with seasons in Hokkaido so always check the specified times at a JTB ofice or at the Midori no Madoguchi ticket window.

Tenninkyo: Tenninkyo, a morning's travel north from Sapporo in the Daisetsuzan National Park, is a quiet, unassuming spa with indoor and outdoor (rotenburo) hot springs, old ramshackle hotels and a stunning waterfall nearby. It is one of *the* places to see the fall colors in Japan. The only thing wild about this place is the beauty of the gorge that surrounds it. The angular rock spires which line the road give a very distinctive feel to this entire area. This area is remote and for probably the first time on this trip you'll be at the end of the road.

Transportation
Tenninkyo is easy to reach. At Asahikawa, walk out of the train station and you'll see a bus stand slightly off to the right on the street. The far right hand stop is for Tenninkyo. The ride is free to hotel guests. The early bus will be full of locals, pretty colorful country folk, returning home from morning shopping. One hour on the bus through magnificent scenery and you're there.

The Daisetsuzan area, although well touristed, doesn't have the public transport you've grown accustomed to in the southern islands. A rental car would be a great way to see this entire area. Without one, buses will have to suffice for reaching the more remote parts of the interior. Explore; just don't do it so late in the day that you can't get a bus back to your lodgings. I've even had good luck hitchhiking, but it's a purely hit-or-miss proposition.

Sightseeing Highlights
▲▲▲ Hike up the valley (with picnic lunch in hand, perhaps), to see the truly gorgeous **Hagoromono Taki**. This waterfall is breathtaking, particularly in autumn. Further up the valley is another falls, unfortunately marred by an inaccessible steel

Post Tour Options 105

bridge that goes up the valley. Walk, enjoy the scenery, and then go back and soak your bones in an outdoor tub (rotenburo).

Lodging
All the hotels in this valley have similar accommodations. The prices are rather high everyplace, due to the limited availability of rooms.

Tenninkyo Grand Hotel (Kamikawa gun, biei cho, Tenninkyo Onzen, Kamikawa. Ph.# 01669-6-2311) has the most extensive bathing facilities. About 10,000 yen per person, two meals and baths included.

Tenninkaku: Tenninkyo-onsen, Higashikawa cho, Kawakumi gun 071-03, Ph.# 0166-97-2111. 10,000 to 15,000 yen.

Return to Sapporo or Go on to Sounkyo

DAY 5: SAPPORO TO SOUNKYO

The transportation on this segment is easy. Stations are small, everything is clearly marked and finding buses is easy. From Tenninkyo to Sounkyo, take the first convenient bus (they run hourly) to Asahikawa. From there get on the first convenient bus up the valley to Sounkyo. There is frequent service on this route and you should have no trouble finding the buses in front of the station.

Fantastic ice-carved rock spires and thin cataracts of water line the Sounkyo Gorge. Everywhere you look there's something magnificent. Fall colors are awesome.

Suggested Schedule

7:00	Check out and off to the station.
8:00	Leave for Asahikawa.
9:41	Arrive in Asahikawa.
9:50	Bus to Sounkyo.
11:40	Arrive in Sounkyo, check into lodgings.
12:00	Ropeway to the top of Mt. Daisetsu, hike for a few hours.
Afternoon	Walk in the park, take a bus into the inner park. Explore. Chujo Setsuri is a spot worth finding as is Lake Mashuko.
Evening	Eat, bathe and relax.

Sightseeing Highlights
On the bus ride, you'll pass **Ryusei no taki** and **Ginga no taki**, two lovely waterfalls.

Take another bus up the canyon from Sounkyo Onzen to **Kobako** and **Obako** ("'Little Box" and "Big Box"; as you might guess, these are box canyons). See the sights early or late in the day without the crowds.

▲▲ **Mt. Daisetsu Ropeway:** 1300 yen gets you a ride to the top of the hill, with a commanding view and great hiking on the ridges behind the ropeway station. Take a picnic lunch and walk. The trails are well marked.

▲▲ **Mashuko:** A small lake in the park, a short bus ride from town, is also a nice place for a picnic.

Last Words

Other places well worth seeing in Hokkaido, given enough time and money, are **Akan National Park**, the **Shakotan Peninsula** near Sapporo, the **Shiretoko Penninsula** on the east coast, and the remote islands of **Rishiri** and **Rebun** on the north coast. Sorry, I can't cover it all in this little book (nor will you be able to in a single trip). J.D. Bisdignani's *Japan Handbook* (Moon Publications) is, to my way of thinking, the best comprehensive guide for Hokkaido.

Returning south to Tokyo by train is simple. Go to the JTB office at Sapporo Eki to book your trip the day before you want to leave. If you plan to fly, get a ticket from the JTB and head for Chitose Airport. After a month of traveling in Japan this will pose no problem for you. By now you know how easy getting around in Japan really is.

JAPANESE FOOD

Visions of raw fish, sea urchin innards and other treats laced with fiery green mustard immediately come to most people's minds when Japanese food is mentioned. To be sure, there are few things the Japanese don't like to eat raw. This, however, is but one facet of a cuisine with phenomenal range and variety.

Entering a restaurant for the first time, the greatest hurdle, even after years in country, is that the menu is unreadable. In some places, you can drag the waitress ouside and point to the plastic mock-up of your selection in the window on the street.

It helps to learn various cuisines and how to recognize the types of restaurants that serve them. Nearly all restaurants in Japan are specialty shops and tend to have a particular "look" about them. They will serve sushi, or tempura, or Chinese food (liberally interpreted), or teppan yaki; seldom will you encounter a place that serves all of them. Finding out what you like takes time and nerve. Time, because there are so many kinds of shops; and nerve, because it means trying things new, unusual, and yes, sometimes gross. Go around peering in doors that may look like you have no business opening them. Don't be intimidated by owners' and clienteles' reactions to you, a foreigner, when you stick your head in the door. It may have been quite some time (if ever) since the last Gaijin stepped in. Usually, the reticent reception at your appearance stems from the owner's fear of serving you poorly, thus embarassing both of you.

When you enter a place for the first time you have to feel it out quickly. In Tokyo they may not bat an eyelid at your appearance, while at a little neighborhood sushi bar in Niigata they may go positively glacial. Nearly anywhere, you can assuage their fears by smiling, doing a light, informal bow and perhaps uttering an appropriate greeting for the time of day.

The main exceptions to this will be some elegant restaurants and private clubs where introductions are necessary for anyone to gain admittance. They just won't let you in. Don't feel badly, you can easily live without those places and their high prices.

Besides the great variety of Japanese food there are many "foreign" food places. Great Indian food, good Italian, French, Vietnamese, Malay and many other kinds are to be found in the larger cities. Don't hesitate to try these places; often their owners are so fanatically dedicated to the type of food they serve that the quality is excellent. Subject to regional variation, the basic types of Japanese food are:

Sushi: Everyone has had this raw fish, seaweed and rice delicacy in the States, but even if you didn't like it here, give it another try in Japan where its preparation is a high art. The best sushi is made with fish just hours old, relatively easy in this island nation. You'll find it is a varied and delightful cuisine. Try some down in the Tsukiji fish market, or on the wharf in Yobuko Town, Kyushu. You might want to avoid it as fast food on trains, etc., where you're unsure about its age, because it can be chewy and generally unappetizing.

Sashimi: This is it: raw fish. Raw, but not unprepared. More effort goes into the slicing, arrangement and preparation of raw goodies than if the same item were cooked. You will be served sashimi for dinner in all ryokan and minshuku, so it's a good idea to learn to like it. Try adding a little lemon juice if the texture is just too... slippery. Add enough lemon juice and it will seem just like cooked fish. The Japanese will slice up anything out of the water and eat it, including the poisonous Fugu fish. Years of schooling are required before one can serve this fish without causing neurological disorders or fatalities. Like to try some? See Rick Kennedy's *Good Tokyo Restaurants*. All other fish and shellfish you'll be served will be safe.

Soba: Noodles. Soba is a slender buckwheat noodle, while its fatter cousin "udon" is made of white flour. Both are served in a delightful broth, just a few degrees the low side of boiling. Add vegetables, tempura shrimp and watercress, a bit of "karashi" (chili pepper) and you have an inexpensive treat that is very sustaining. The Chinese noodle "ramen" is a slender noodle often fried and mixed with meat and vegetables—very tasty. Noodles, particularly soba, are the staple foods of the traveler because they are served in stations throughout the land.

Teppan Yaki: Benihana food—meats, fish and vegetables cooked on hot steel. When you just have to have a steak, this is where you'll find a good one. Usually delicious, always expensive.

Yakitori: Chicken kebabs, pretty simple and very good. Available everywhere, these (cooked) tidbits are popular with Gaijin and Japanese alike. Order some with sauce (tare) and some grilled with salt (shioyaki). The chef always has some new variations going. Look at what fellow diners order and don't be afraid to request the same by way of a little judicious pointing.

Okonomiyaki: Popular in the Kansai or Osaka area, this "Japanese pizza" of flour, egg, cabbage and various meats and usually some squid is grilled on teppan (steel) and covered with shaved dried fish and sosu. Sosu (sauce), on the tables in most smaller restaurants, is made of tomato ketchup and worchestershire sauce. You will sometimes find it served on yatai late at night in Tokyo.

Yatai: Street carts, the salvation of late night drinkers and anyone who loves midnight snacks. These small carts appear after dark in towns accross the land, serving everything from octopus balls (takoyaki) to roasted chestnuts and oden, a mixture of fish cakes, cabbage, tofu and whatever else is in stock tonight. The chestnut cart vendors roam the streets on winter nights with a plaintive wail of song and haunting pipe music.

Sukiyaki: Japanese stew, great in cold weather. Finely sliced, well marbled beef, onions, scallions, mushrooms, bamboo shoots and more in a broth of sake, soya and sugar. The ingredients are cooked as you eat and then dipped in whipped raw egg. The egg is optional but who'd want to pass it by? It really makes the dish, and if you can't stand the thought, order something else.

Tempura: Vegetables of all sorts as well as fish and or shrimp dipped in a light, slightly crunchy batter, served absolutely sizzling hot. Outstanding tempura is hard to find, but even run-of-the-mill quality is quite edible.

Kaiseki Ryori: The epitomy of Japanese cuisine to most people. Of extraordinary variety and delicacy, kaiseki ryori is designed to be eaten before the tea ceremony. Many small portions are served in a pre-determined sequence. Good ryokan frequently serve a version of it for dinner. Kyoto Ryori is a variation you'll enjoy when you get to that city.

Inaka Ryori: Country inn style food. A variety of foods cooked over charcoal and served with sauces and whatever the cook finds appropriate. Kushiyaki is a variation you'll find in the town of Niigata.

Kushikatsu: Pork and or chicken fried in a batter and served with mountains of cabbage and sosu. Cheap and good, it is often found in subterranean shopping center/train stations.

Tonkatsu: Crispy breaded pork cutlet served with a scrumptious barbecue-like sosu and salad. I love it.

Teishoku: This type of meal can be a number of things such as tonkatsu or katsu (beef), served as a "plate" with rice, soup and a salad. A good way to order lunch. Ask for "Katsu teishoku kudasai."

Seto: Workingman's lunch. Small restaurants in average neighborhoods usually have a set lunch (ranchi seto), the special of the day. More food for less cash.

Vikingu: Viking as in smorgasbord or breakfast buffet. Served in most western-style hotels and business hotels, you can eat enough to get you through the day for a very reasonable price. The spread usually includes both western and Japanese foods. Take advantage of these when possible.

Kissaten: Coffee shops. These are everywhere and oh so nice when you need them. Foreigners always remark on the astronomical price of coffee in Japan. In these small, comfortable little shops you're paying for a place to sit down and get away from it all for a while. The coffee is expensive to pay the high rent. They have small libraries of newspapers and manga (comic books) to take the worker's mind off his cares while he rests. The coffee is usually fantastic.

McDonalds: We all know what these are. The Japanese love them. They can provide you a link to home when gastronomic culture shock strikes. Best of all, they almost always have bathrooms.

FOOD VOCABULARY

O-ohan   rice specifically, food in general
Nikku   meat (usually beef)
Bekon   bacon
Hamu   ham
Buta nikku   pork
Rosu   roast beef (but not what you think—usually a tough fatty piece of meat fried and served as tonkatsu; in good places it's good.)
Tori   chicken (literally, bird)

O-sushi   sushi
Sakana   fish
Kani   crab
Ebi   shrimp
Oki ebi   lobster
Unagi   eel
Uni   sea urchin
Ikka   squid
Maguro   tuna
Hammachi   yellow tail
Kaki   oysters
Hamaguri   clam

Japanese Food

Wasabi   horseradish mustard
O-shoyu   soy sauce
Sosu   Japanese sauce with ketchup and worcestershire

Yasai   vegetables
Gohan   rice
Tamanegi   onion
Kuri   cucumber
Retasu   lettuce
Kinoko   mushroom (generic)
Shitake   a fine white mushroom
Kabetsu   cabbage
Take no ko   bamboo shoots
Ninjin   carrot
Jagaimo   potato
Ninnikku   garlic
Remon   lemon
Meron   melon (expensive)
Ringo   apple (can be very expensive; try Fuji ringos)
Orenji   orange
Mikan   Japanese orange (good)
Ichigo   strawberry

Sato   sugar
Hachimitsu   honey

Pan   bread
Tamago   eggs
Bata   butter
Tosto   toast
Pinatsu bata   peanut butter
Jamu   jam
Mixto sando   Japanese tea sandwiches
Sandoichi   sandwich
Kare raisu   curry rice

O-mizu   water
Sumetai mizu   cold water
O-yu   hot water
O-cha   green tea, no caffeine
Ban-cha   tea made with roasted rice
Ko-cha   regular Chinese tea with caffeine
Miruku   milk
Kurimu   cream
Jusu   juice
Beeru   beer

O-sake   liquor, especially rice wine
Wainu   wine (skip it)
Mizu wari   scotch and water, the national drink
Sho chu   rice liquor
Shochu remon   shochu cocktail, lemony
Bancha wari   a popular hot drink in Hokkaido made with bancha and shochu
Masu zake   cold sake in a cedar box
Kora   cola

BRIEF HISTORY OF JAPAN

Japan, once part of the Asian mainland, fell off into the Pacific (as some people predict California will) in a series of earthquakes about 20,000 ago. Anthropologists believe early people migrated to the islands across land bridges from Korea and Siberia during the last Ice Age, as well as by boat from Polynesia.

100-600 AD: Jimmu Tenno, the semi-mythical emperor who was the Japanese counterpart to Britain's King Arthur, formed a kingdom called Yamato, with its capitol somewhere between Kyoto and Nara—it was customary to move the capitol each time an emperor died. The Japanese racial identity dates from the Yamato Period, as do the Shinto religion, the subservience of women, and ritual bathing.

The **Geku** or Outer Shrine at Ise dates back to the Yamato Period—478 A.D.; the **Naiku** or Inner Shrine is even older, built in the year 5 B.C.

600-794: The imperial bureaucracy had become too large to relocate upon the emperor's death, and the first permanent capitol was established in **Nara**. The **Horyu-ji** (oldest intact Buddhist temple in Japan), **Kasuga Shrine** and **Kokuho-kan** (Treasure Hall) were built during the Nara Period. Buddhism was declared to be the national religion, and in 756 AD the **Todaiji Temple** and its **Daibutsu** (Great Buddha) were completed. Just 28 years later the new emperor, Kammu, decided to move the capitol from Nara to Kyoto. Also built during this period were the original **Asakusa-Kannon Temple**, the reconstruction of which can be seen in Tokyo, and the **Futaarasan Shrine** at Nikko.

794-1182: The 400-year Heian Period, while the capitol was in **Kyoto**, saw the empire expand rapidly to control most of modern-day Japan. The emperors devoted most of their time to studying Buddhism, art and literature, while the land was actually ruled by competing aristocratic families (notably the Fujiwara family) through shoguns (generals) and samurai (warriors). Also in this period, a peculiarly Japanese theology evolved which held that the ancient Shinto gods were manifestations of the Buddha, therefore people could be Shinto and Buddhist at the same time.

Kofukuji Temple and **Kasuga Shrine** in Nara were originally built by the Fujiwara family in 710 and belonged to them throughout the Heian Period; the temple has been destroyed and faithfully reconstructed twice. **Itsukushima Shrine** at Miyajima also dates back to this period.

1182-1543: Japan's capitol moved to Kamakura, just south of modern-day Tokyo, where the great shogun Yoritomo Minamoto, and later his sons, ruled. In 1281, Kublai Khan invaded Japan with a force of more than 100,000 Mongol soldiers. Accompanying Kublai Khan was Marco Polo, who later described Japan for the first time to European readers. During a great battle at **Hakata** a typhoon struck, sweeping both Mongol and Japanese armies into the sea and ending the invasion. The typhoon was called "Kamikaze" ("Divine wind").

The rulers at Kamakura failed to pay the surviving samurai and lost their allegiance, and Japan plunged into a series of civil wars. In 1335 Emperor Godaigo took control of part of the army, but three years later shogun Takauji Ashikaga drove the emperor into the mountains and formed his own court at Kyoto. Many of Kyoto's great pavilions and temples were built during this Muromachi Period (1335-1572) by Takauji and his successors. After Takauji's death warlords struggled in continuous civil war for over 100 years.

1543-49: The first Portuguese ships arrived in Japan, bringing Catholic missionaries who attempted to manipulate the warlords against each other and competed with the Buddhists for power. The Europeans also brought firearms, a few of which they sold to the warlords at astonishingly high prices. Within a few years the Japanese had copied the new technology and were producing good quality guns of their own. (Sound familiar?)

1573-1600: Civil strife continued as powerful warlords, particularly Nobunaga Oda and his successor Toyotomi Hideyoshi (who built Miyajima's **Hall of a Thousand Mats**), struggled unsuccessfully to restore the shogunate. During this era, the Azuchi-Momoyama Period, Japan's greatest castles were built or expanded (the **Castle of the White Heron** in Himeji was first built in the 14th century, but reached its present massive size during the Azuchi-Momoyama Period) and firearms were first used in warfare. It was also a time of bold artistic development, including popularization of **Kabuki** theater and the chanoyu (tea ceremony).

1603-1867: The Edo Period began when Ieyasu Tokugawa conquered all rivals to become the most powerful shogun in Japanese history. He moved the government to the fortified town of Edo, later renamed Tokyo. Missionaries and traders from Europe were arriving in increasing numbers (These included William Adams, the prototype for "Anjin-san," hero of the best-selling though historically inaccurate novel *Shogun*, who lived in the town of Ito on the Izu Peninsula). Meanwhile, several Japanese warlords converted to Christianity and sent emissaries to the Pope in Rome by way of Mexico. A Jesuit-inspired insurrection, combined with concern that a Papal bull dividing colonization rights to the entire world between Spain and Portugal might mean attempts to colonize Japan, led the shogun to banish all Europeans. Only the Dutch, who were not Roman Catholics, were allowed a small trading colony on Dejima Island in Nagisaki Harbor; this island was Japan's only contact with western civilization for over two centuries.

Ieyasu Tokugawa built the **Nijo Castle** (1603) and **Kiyomizu Terra**(1633), both in Kyoto. Nikko's **Rinnoji Temple** and **Sacred Bridge** (built on the site where earlier sacred bridges had existed since antiquity) date from the same period, as does the **Kompira Shrine** at Kotohira. The incident of the "47 Ronin," commemorated by **Sengakuji Temple** in Tokyo, occurred in 1703.

The Edo Period was one of "law and order" in the extreme. Large numbers of samurai were stationed throughout the country to prevent opponents from organizing against the shogunate. They also oppressed the peasants, victimizing them with impunity and sometimes executing people for "crimes" of disrespect or bad manners. There were no wars, internal or external, and many samurai became wandering soldiers of fortune, while others became dandys more skilled in the tea ceremony than in the martial arts. Meanwhile, the nation's wealth became concentrated in the rising merchant class. By the early 19th century the shogun lacked power to do anything besides exploit his peasantry.

Then ships from the west started arriving again.

Russian traders to Hokkaido came first, followed by a fleet of American "black ships" under the command of Admiral Perry, who opened trade with Japan by threat of force. When a trade agreement was signed with the U.S. in 1853 and Townsend Harris became the first American ambassador to Japan, several European nations sought to establish trade relations in the same way: by force. British ships bombarded Kagoshima in 1863, and the following year a joint British, Dutch and French fleet invaded. His weakness obvious to the people of Japan, the shogun's power collapsed.

At Shimoda on the Izu Peninsula you'll see **Hofukuji Temple**, dedicated to U.S. Ambassador Harris' Japanese mistress.

1867-1912: The Imperial family, which had survived in powerless seclusion behind palace walls in Kyoto for 250 years, suddenly became the only semblance of government in Japan—and the only leadership with whom the outside world could establish diplomatic relations. In 1867 Emperor Meiji, often called "the monarch of modern Japan," ascended the throne. Meiji promptly moved the Imperial Court to the shogunate capital of Edo, renamed the capital city Tokyo (which means "eastern capital"), declared Shinto the state religion (one of its tenets being that the Emperor was divine and his decrees infallible), abolished the feudal samurai system and declared the warlords' holdings forfeit to the Emperor—quite a coup, considering that few people had even realized Japan still *had* an emperor.

Meiji ruled for 45 years, during which time Japan enthusiastically embraced western science—telephones, electric lights and that most powerful symbol of modern technology, railroads. Many Japanese scholars (including the artists exhibited at the **Bridgestone Museum**) traveled to the Europe to study, and it became fashionable for Japanese men to marry Gaijin women. Japan also began to emerge as a military power and waged war outside her own borders for the first time. Winning wars against China (1894-95) and Russia (1904-05), Japan gained control over the island of Formosa and portions of the Asian mainland.

Tokyo's **Meiji Shrine** was built soon after the Emperor's death in 1912.

1912-1925: Upon Meiji's death, his son Taisho took the imperial throne. Taisho became ill and was rarely seen, but capable ministers ruled in his name. Japan entered World War I on the side of the Allies and continued to develop military strength. After the war, relations with the U.S. deteriorated, largely because the U.S. passed laws denying American citizenship to the growing number of Japanese immigrants and restricting them from buying or owning land. In 1923 the Kanto Earthquake struck Japan, destroying much of Tokyo and Yokohama and killing over 100,000 people. It was the worst natural disaster of modern times.

1926-45: Hirohito, who had studied and traveled extensively in Europe before becoming Emperor, adapted the militaristic attitudes of pre-WWII Europe. Japan's growing military power was patterned after that of Germany. Beginning in 1931, Japan expanded her empire by invading Manchuria and China. In 1940 Japan officially made an alliance with Hitler's Germany. By bombing Pearl Harbor late in 1941, Japan became locked in a four-year-long death struggle with the U.S. which raged across most of the Pacific Ocean until, in 1945, the U.S. dropped atomic bombs on Hiroshima and Nagasaki, and Japan surrendered. **Peace Park** in Hiroshima memorializes the victims of the world's first sample of nuclear war.

1946-present: After World War II ended, the Japanese faced starvation, economic ruin and military occupation by the U.S. and the U.S.S.R. The U.S. poured reconstruction funds into Japan in unprecedented amounts, and this financing together with the fanatical work ethic of the Japanese people created an industrial base which has come to rival even that of the U.S. Today Japan, with no military capability, has emerged as the second-greatest industrial power in the world, stronger economically than any European, Arabic or Communist nation. Japan's government today is a constitutional monarchy. The seat of government is in the National Diet, in central Tokyo across from the Imperial Palace. The Emperor, a figurehead much like the Queen of England with limited real power, belongs to the unbroken line of Emperors that can be traced back to the same time as the Roman Empire in Europe.

The **Imperial Palace** in Tokyo, which was destroyed by firebombing during World War II, was rebuilt during the 1960s using modern materials and traditional architecture.

LANGUAGE

You can get by as a tourist in Japan speaking virtually no Japanese at all—but you will enjoy yourself much more if you learn a little of the language.

Imagine for a moment...

On the train from Niigata to Bandai you notice an old Japanese man looking at you intently.

You take a deep breath and say in your best Japanese, "Konnichi wa."

The old gentleman simply smiles, ducks his head in an informal bow, and keeps smiling.

Feeling a bit awkward, you search for something more to say. "Doko e ikimasuka?" you ask. (Where are you going?)

Your new friend completely ignores this. He wags a finger at you. "Nihongo o jozu desu ne?!" (You speak Japanese very well, don't you?")

"Iie, Nihongo dekimasen," you say. (No I can't speak Japanese.)

Ignoring this as well, the old guy asks, "Dochira kara?" (Where are you from?)

"Amerika-jin desu." (I'm American.)

"Ah, Amerika e itan deshoo!" (I've been to America). Then he names the places he visited: San Furanshisuko, Rosu Anjeresu, Niyu Yoku, Rasu Vegasu, Gurando Kanyon, Disunirando. He sucks air between his teeth, shakes his head and adds, "Yokatta na!" (That was wonderful.)

The train arrives at the old man's village, surrounded by ragged high mist-shrouded mountains. It looks just like your fantasies of Japan.

The old man gathers his scarf-wrapped big-city purchases. Ready, he smiles, pats you on the arm, bows and toddles out the door onto the silent platform.

As the diesel train chugs out of the station into the next set of climbing curves, you think how lucky you are. Unlike your fellow Americans locked inside package tours, you're free to touch Japan on its own terms. The old man, a short conversation, the village in its valley have reached you. Now, you feel, you've truly been in Japan.

A vocabulary of just ten words made it possible.

What's that you say? *Nihongo dekimasen?*
Read on...

Pronunciation

Japanese is a difficult language, no two ways about it. But at least, unlike some others such as Chinese, it is easily pronounceable. Once you learn the basic sounds of the language, you should be able to read words from a dictionary or phrasebook and say them so that they will be intelligible to the average man on the street.

The vowels, predominant in Japanese, are the key to pronunciation. Nearly all words end with a vowel or an 'n' sound.

A: pronounced as in "Ahh" at the doctors office.
E: the e is pronounced as in left.
I: pronounced as "ee" as in "eek, a mouse!"
O: a regular o as in "Oh, I just love your new pearls!"
U: sounds like the "u" in lunatic.

The "n" sound is a long drawn out nnnn... as if you were saying thoughtfully, "Nnno... I don't think so".

Other sounds that give Gaijin trouble are "tsu" and the "r" sounds "ra," "ri," "ru," "re" and "ro." "Tsu" is a "su" sound with a soft touch of "t" at the beginning. Pronounce it starting with your tongue at the roof of your mouth and touching the tops of your front teeth. The 'r' sound in Japanese is slightly rolled as in Spanish. If you can't manage that feat of linguistic prestidigitation, don't worry about it overly much; it won't keep you from being understood.

The biggest trick to correct Japanese pronounciation is: Stress all syllables equally. Say "sa-ya-no-ra," not "SAY-a-NOR-a."

Using a Phrasebook

Mentally practice saying words you read in a phrasebook to yourself a couple of times before you blurt them out. Short words should give you little trouble; longer ones may take a little more time to master. Learn a few. Some phrases will be used over and over again on a daily basis and you'll remember them in short order.

The biggest problem with a phrasebook is that while it may help you ask questions, the answers come at nearly the speed of light and likely as not, are completely unintelligible. Try to have an idea of what kind of answer to expect and be waiting for it. For example, when asking directions, the answer is quite likely to contain words such as north, south, east and west, up and down, right, left, elevator or stairs.

Japanese Grammar

It's nothing like English, and way beyond the scope of even a full phrasebook. Personal pronouns such as "I" and "you" are at the beginning of a sentence (usually); object nouns, participles and all the rest go in the middle, while the verbs tend to bunch up at the end of the sentence. Learn a few phrases by rote and let the general structure sink in as you go along.

Reading Japanese

Japanese "letters" represent syllables. The written syllabaries of *hiragana* (used for all Japanese words) and *katakana* (used for foreign words) sound like this: "a, i, u, e, o, ka, ki, ku, ke, ko, sa, shi, su, se, so, ta, chi, tsu, te, to . ." etc. You could learn both in a week if you set your mind to it, and that would let you to read things like menus and train station signs, not exactly relieving your illiteracy but at least taking the edge off it. Hiragana and katakana are both contained in appendices to most small dictionaries. If you become familiar with all the sounds in the syllabaries, you will have Japanese pronunciation down pat.

Here are some words and phrases you'll find useful in your travels:

Yes Hai *(hi)*
No Iie. *(ee ye)*

Numbers

1	iichi
2	ni
3	san
4	shi (becomes "yon" after ten)
5	go
6	roku
7	shichi or nana
8	hachi
9	ku
10	ju
11	juiichi
12	juni
13	jusan
14	juyon
15	jugo
16	juroku
17	jushichi
18	juhachi
19	juku
20	niju
21	niju iichi
22	niju ni
23	niju san
24	niju yon
	(and so on, adding numbers to the word for twenty.)

30	sanju
	(37 would be three tens seven, sanju nana—confusing at first but really very simple.)
40	yonju
50	goju
60	rokuju
70	nanaju
80	hachiju
90	kuju
100	hyaku
110	hyaku ju
115	hyaku ju go
120	hyaku niju
130	hyaku sanju
200	nihyaku
300	sanbyaku
400	yonhyaku
500	gohyaku
600	rophyaku
700	nanahyaku
800	hapyaku
900	kuhyaku
1000	sen
1150	sen hyaku goju
2000	nisen
3000	sansen
4000	yonsen
5000	gosen
6000	rokusen
7000	nanasen
8000	hasen
9000	kusen
10,000	iichiman
50,000	goman
80,000	hachiman
100,000	juman
1,000,000	hyakuman
10,000,000	senman
100,000,000	iichioku
	(If you need to say iichioku, consider hiring me as your personal tour-guide-for-life.)

Dates

January	iichigatsu
February	nigatsu
March	sangatsu
April	shigatsu
May	gogatsu
June	rokugatsu
July	shichigatsu
August	hachigatsu
September	kugatsu
October	jugatsu
November	juiichigatsu
December	junigatsu

(Note that the months are numbered instead of named. June 21 is "rokugatsu niju iichi niichi" ("Sixth month, twenty first day"). In this context "niichi" means "day.")

Days of the Week

Sunday	Nichiyobi
Monday	Getsuyobi
Tuesday	Kayobi
Wednesday	Suiyobi
Thursday	Mokuyobi
Friday	Kinyobi
Saturday	Doyobi

Seasons

Spring	Haru
Summer	Natsu
Fall	Aki
Winter	Fuyu

Times

Morning	asa
Afternoon	hiru
Evening	yube
Night	yoru
This morning	kesa
Today	kiyo
Tonight	konban
Now	ima
Later	ato de
Before	mae ni
Tomorrow	ashita

Yesterday	kino
Day after tomorrow	asatte
Day before yesterday	ototoi
This year	kotoshi
Next year	rainen
Last year	kyonen

The most important words in any language are those that ask how to say the next word you might need. Rather than look every word up in the dictionary, it's easier to point at something and say, "what is that in Japanese?"

Nihongo de kore wa nan desuka? What is this in Japanese? (literally, "Japanese in, this is what?")
Nihongo de 'rice' wa nan to yu imi desuka? How do you say "rice" in Japanese?
Nihongo de, rice wa gohan desu. In Japanese, rice is "gohan."

Two words appear at the end of many Japanese sentences: "desu" and "desuka" (pronounced "des" and "deska." The u sound is nearly silent.) "Desuka" makes a sentence into a question:
Kore wa nan desuka? What is this?
Kore wa Gohan desu. This is rice.
Without the "ka," "desu" is the equivalent of the word "is" in English. It also serves as emphasis, ending a sentence firmly:
Kore wa hon desu. This is a book.

Other verbs also become questions when "-ka" is added to the end:
How much? Ikura desuka?
You can get the price of nearly anything you can point to simply by saying, "ikura desuka?"
Equally important when shopping for tourist type items such as cameras and watches, is the phrase:
Can you give me a discount? Waribiki dekimasuka?

Can you . . . ? . . . dekimasuka?
Can you speak English? Eigo ga dekimasuka?
Can you speak Japanese? Nihongo ga dekimasuka?
Yes, I can. Hai dekimaso.
No, I can't speak Japanese. Iie, Nihongo ga dekimasen.
("Iie," pronounced "ee-ye," means no. "Nihon" means "Japan" and "go" means language, so "Nihongo" is "Japanese." "Eikoku" is "England," so "Eigo" means "English.")

Do you have. . . ? . . .arimasuka?
Do you have sushi? Sushi ga arimasuka?
Do you have a room? Heya ga arimasuka?
Yes, we do. Hai, heya ga arimasu.
We have no room. Iie, heya ga arimasen.
(By adding the "-sen" suffix, the verb becomes negative. Another way of saying "We have no room" is "Chotto main desu." This really means, "We are a little full." A polite way of saying the same unpleasant thing.)

Where is. . . ? Doko desuka?
Where is the toilet? Toirei wa doko desuka?
Where is the station? Eki wa doko desuka?
Where is a policeman? Keisatsu wa doko desuka?
Where is a hotel? Oteru wa doko desuka?
Where is a minshuku? Minshuku wa doko desuka?
Where is a bank? Ginko wa doko desuka?
Where is the bus stop? Basu tei wa doko desuka?

"Kudasai" means "please" or "to receive." You can ask for all kinds of things with this handy word:
Tempura noodles, please. Tempura soba kudasai.
Ramen noodles, please. Ramen kudasai.
Coffee, please. Kohii kudasai.

Good Ii
Is it good? (or) Is it all right? Ii desuka?
Often a solicitous housemother will ask, "Iiii?" "Good? Is everything alright?"
Yes it is fine (good). Hai, ii desu.

Delicious Oishi
Your host will look at you and say "Oishi?" This means "Do you like it? Is it good?"
If you like it say "Oishi."
If you *really* like it, try "Sugoku oishi." ("Very delicious.")
If it is not delicious, say "Oishikunai." (The "nai" at the end of "oishi" does the same as "sen" on "dekimasen"—it makes a negative. "Not delicious." *Very* seldom would a Japanese person come right out and say "Oishikunai.")

Some More Food Words

Chopsticks	o-hashi
Sweet (or) delicious	amai
Sour	Supai
Spicy hot	karai

Bitter	nigai
Flavor	aji
Hot	atsui
Cold (food or drink)	sumetai
	("Cold" (weather) is "samui")
I'm hungry	Onaka suita (My stomach is empty)
I'm thirsty	Nodo ga itai (My throat hurts)
I'm full	Onaka ipai

Lodging Words

Hotel	oteru
Minshuku	minshuku
Ryokan	ryokan
Japanese room	washitsu
Western-style room	yoshitsu
Room w/ two meals	nishoku
Room charge	ryokin
Reservation	yoyaku
Room	heya
Bathroom (toilet)	toirei
Bath	o-furo
Japanese food	Nihon shoku
Western food	yushoku
Towel	tauru ("ta-u-ru")
Slippers	suripa

Terrain Words

Mountain	yama
River	kawa
Peninsula	hanto
Cape	zaki
Town	machi
City	shi
Road	doro
Bay	wan
Island	shima

Transportation Words

Plane	hikoki
Bus	basu
Boat	fune
Car	kuruma (or) jidosha
Train	densha
Subway	chikatetsu
Walk	aruite
Taxi	takushi

Greetings

Good morning	Ohio gozaimasu
Good day	Konichi wa
Good evening	Kon ban wa
Good night	Oyasuminasai
How do you do	Hajimemashite
Pleased to meet you	Yoroshiku
Goodbye	Sayonara
Thanks	Domo
Thank you	Arigato
Thank you very much	Domo arigato gozaimashita
Please	Kudasai
Please help, do a favor	Onegai shimasu (literally, "I beg you")
See you later	Sore ja, mata ne
Excuse me	Gomen nasai (or) Sumimasen
I've been rude, imposed	Shitsurei shimasu (or) O jama shimashita

Health

Hurt(s)	itai
Sick	byoki
Headache	atama ga itai
Stomach ache	onaka ga itai
Sore throat	nodo ga itai
Please help me	tetsudaite kudasai
Doctor	isha (or) sensei
Drug store	kusuriya
Medicine	kusuri
Hospital	byooin
Ambulance	kyukyusha
Body	karada
Eye	me
Ear	mimi
Nose	hana
Mouth	kuchi
Arm	ude
Leg	ashi

General

Telephone	denwa
International telephone	kokusai denwa (dial 0051)
Just a moment	chotto matte

Hey!	ano ne!
No smoking car	kinnen sha
Fast/slow	haiyai/yukuri
Hot/cold	atsui/samui
Near/far	chikai/toi
Big/small	okii/chisai
Long/short	nagai/michikai
Narrow/wide	semai/hiroi
Love/hate	ai/kirai
Cheap/expensive	yasui/takai
Beautiful	kirei
Wonderful	subarashi
Great!	sugoi
Full/empty	ipai/suite imasu
Drunk	yopparai
Happy/sad	shiawase/sabishi
Healthy	genki (also used as a greeting among friends: "Genki?-Genki yo!")
Good/bad	ii/dame
Delicious/tastless	oishi/mazui
Sleep	nemuri
I want to sleep	Nemutai
Shop (store)	mise
Museum	hakubutsukan
Book store	hon ya san
Restaurant	shokudo

Directions

Up	ue ("oo-e")
Down	shita
Right	migi
Left	hidari
In front of	mae ri
In back of	ushiro ni
North	kita
South	minami
West	nishi
East	higashi
Stairs	kaidan
Elevator	erebeta

YOUTH HOSTELS

Youth hostels offer a low-price lodging alternative to those travelers willing to sacrifice privacy and comfort in favor of budget. Accommodations are dormitory-style, and guests must provide their own sheets or rent them at an additional charge. The price at most Japanese youth hostels is 2700 yen per night. The maximum stay is three consecutive nights. Reservations are strongly advised.

There is no maximum age limit; if you do not already have the required membership card from an IYH hostel in another country, you can get one for 3000 yen at the Japan Youth Hostels national office, Hoken Kaikan, 1-1, Sadohara-cho, Ichigaya, Shinjuku-ku, Tokyo 162. They can also provide a complete list of hostels in Japan.

Youth hostels convenient to the tour route suggested in this book include:

TOKYO
Tokyo International Youth Hostel, 21-1 Kakuragashi, Shinjuku-ku, Ph# 235-1107.

IZU PENINSULA (SHIMODA)
Gensu Youth Hostel, Ph# 05586-2-0035, 25 minutes from Shimoda Eki by bus.

ISE AREA
Youth Hostel Kontaiji, 3-24-1 Toba, Ph# (0599) 25-3035. Short walk from Toba Eki. Men only.

KYOTO
Higashiyama Youth Hostel, 112, Shirakawabashi-goken-cho, Sanjo-dori, Higashiyama-ku, Kyoto 605, Ph# 761-8135. 20 minutes from Kyoto Eki by bus.

NARA
Nara Youth Hostel, 1716 Horencho, Ph# 22-1334.

KOTOHIRA
Youth Hostel Kotohira Seinen-No-Ie, 1241, Kawanishi-otsu, Kotohira-machi, Nakatado-gun, Kagawa-ken 766, Ph# (08777) 3-3836. Short walk from Kotohira Eki.

HIROSHIMA
Hiroshima Youth Hostel, 1-13-6, Ushita-shin-machi, Higashi-ku, Hiroshima City 730, Ph# (082) 221-5343. 10-minute bus ride from Hiroshima Eki.

HATOMIZAKI
 None. See "National Citizens Hotel" information in Day 13.

SADO ISLAND
 Hosen kan Youth Hostel, 1111 Katagami, Niibo-mura, Sado-gun, Niigata Pref., Ph# 025942-3125.

URA-BANDAI
 Ura-bandai Youth Hostel, Goshikinuma, Ura-bandai, Azuma-kyoku, Fukushima-ken 969-27, Ph# (024132) 2811.

KANAZAWA
 Kanazawa Youth Hostel, Ph# 0762-52-3414.

NIKKO:
 Nikko Youth Hostel, 2854, Tokorono, Nikko City, Ph# 0288-54-1013.

FESTIVALS

ALL JAPAN
January 1   Ganjitsu (New Year's Day)
January 2-6   Daruma Ichi, good luck dolls sold at temples
February 3   Setsubun (Bean-Throwing Festival) at many temples
March 3   Hinamatsuri (Doll Festival)
Spring   Cherry Blossom Festival starts early April in the south, moves north through early May
May 5   Kodomo-No-Hi (Children's Day)
July 7   Tanabata (Star Festival)
July 13-16   O-Bon Festival (crowded everywhere!)
August   National vacation season (crowded everywhere!)
Autumn   Fall colors start early October in Hokkaido, move south through November
November 15   Shichi-go-san (Children's Visiting Day at shrines)
December 31   Joya-No-Kane (New Year's Eve)

AOMORI
August 1-7   Nebuta Matsuri Festival

FUKUOKA
May 3-4   Hakata Dontaku Festival, parade
July 15   Hakata Yamagasa Festival

HIMEJI
October 14-15   Kenka Matsuri Festival, Matsubara Shrine

HIROSHIMA
August 6   Peace Ceremony, Peace Memorial Park

ISE
April 5-8   Kagura-sai, Ise Shrines

KARATSU
November 2-4   Okunchi Festival, Karatsu Shrine

KYOTO
May 15   Aoi Matsuri (Hollyhock Festival), Shimogamo and Kamigamo Shrines
May, third Sunday   Mifune Matsuri Festival, Oi River
July 16-17   Gion Matsuri, parade
August 16   Daimonji Bonfire, Mt. Nyoigatake
October 22   Jidai Matsuri (Festival of Eras), Heian Shrine, procession; Fire Festival, Yuki Shrine, Kurama
December 31   Okera Mairi Ceremony, Yasaka Shrine

Festivals

LAKE AKAN, HOKKAIDO
October 8-10   Marimo Matsuri

MIYAJIMA
Mid-July   Kangensai Music Festival, Itsukushima Shrine

NARA
January 15   Grass Fire Ceremony on Mt. Wakakusayama
February 3   Lantern Festival, Kasuga Shrine
March 13   Kasuga Festival, Kasuga Shrine
December 17   On-Matsuri Festival, Kasuga Shrine, procession

NIKKO
May 17-18   Grand Festival, Toshogu Shrine
April 16-17   Yayoi Matsuri, Futaarasan Shrine, procession
October 17   Autumn Festival, Toshogu Shrine

MORIOKA
June 15   Chagu-Chagu Umakko (Horse Festival)

OSAKA
June 14   Rice-Planting Festival, Sumiyoshi Shrine

SAPPORO
February 5-9   Snow Festival

TOKYO
January 6   Dezomeshiki (New Year's Parade of Firemen)
April 29   Emperor's Birthday, Imperial Palace
Late April   Festivals at Yasukuni and Meiji Shrines
May, third weekend   Sanja Matsuri Festival, Asakusa Shrine
June 1-2   Hanashobu (Iris Exhibition), Meiji Shrine
June 10-16   Sanno Festival, Hie Shrine
Late September-Early October   Grand Tokyo Festival, parades
October 11-13   Oeshiki Festival, Hommonji Temple
October 31-November 3   Autumn Festival, Meiji Shrine
Mid-November   Tori-no-ichi (Rake Fair), Otori Shrines
Mid-December   Hagoita-Ichi Fair (Year-End Market), Asakusa Kannon Temple

For a complete listing of trade fairs and shows throughout Japan, get a copy of "Exhibitions, Fairs & Events in Japan" from any Japan National Tourist Organization office.

DIRECTORY

INFORMATION SOURCES
Japan National Tourist Organization is your best advance information source. Write any office and they'll keep your mailbox full of brochures, pamphlets and newsletters. Call them to ask questions and get specific advice.
Tokyo: 2-10-1 Yuraku-cho, Chiyoda-ku, Tokyo 100, Japan.
Ph# (03)-216-1902.
New York: 630 Fifth Ave., New York NY 10111.
Ph# (212)-757-5640.
Chicago: 333 N. Michigan Ave., Chicago IL 60601,
Ph# (312)-332-3975.
Dallas: 1519 Main St., Suite 200, Dallas TX 75201,
Ph# (214)-741-4931.
San Francisco: 1737 Post St., San Francisco CA 94115,
Ph# (415)-931-0700.
Los Angeles: 624 S. Grand Ave., Los Angeles CA 90017,
Ph# (808)-923-7631.
Honolulu: 2270 Kalakaua Ave., Honolulu HI 96815,
Ph# (808)-923-7631.
Canada: 165 University Ave., Toronto, Ont. M5H 3B8,
Ph# (416)-366-7140.
Great Britain: 167 Regent St., London W 1,
Ph# 734-9638.
Australia: 115 Pitt St., Sydney, N.S.W. 2000,
Ph# 232-4522.
Hong Kong: Peter Bldg., 58 Queen's Road Central,
Ph# 5-227913.

IN JAPAN
Japan Travel-Phone, a free English-language information service for travelers in Japan, can help with language difficulties and give advice on good restaurants and accommodations. Until recently you had to go through a telephone operator (who often spoke no English) to call the Travel-Phone. Now you can dial direct (9:00-17:00 daily):
Eastern Japan: (0120)-222-800
Western Japan: (0120)-444-800
Tokyo JNTO: 502-1461
Kyoto JNTO: 371-5649

Japan Association of Travel Agents will handle complaints about services provided by its members. Contact them at Zen-Nittu Kasumigaseki Building, 3-3-3, Kasumigaseki, Chiyoda-ku, Tokyo 100, Japan. Ph# (03)-592-1271.

ABOUT THE AUTHOR

David Old has visited Japan fifteen times as a student, traveler, writer and motorcycle racer, attended Kansai Gaikoku Gaidai University in Osaka, and spent over two years exploring the country. When not traveling, he resides in Santa Fe, New Mexico where he operates a charter helicopter service. His previous book is *How to Keep Your Honda ATC Big Red Alive*, co-authored with Richard Sealey.

JMP TRAVELERS CATALOG

All Items Field Tested, Highly Recommended, Completely Guaranteed and Discounted Below Retail.

Combination Rucksack/
Suitcase . . . . $70.00 postpaid

At 9" x 21" x 13", this specially designed, sturdy, functional bag is maximum carry-on-the-plane size. (Fits under the seat.) Constructed by Jesse Ltd. of rugged waterproof nylon Cordura material, with hide-away shoulder straps, waist belt (for use as a ruck sack) and top and side handles and a detachable shoulder strap (for toting as a suitcase). Perimeter zippers allow easy access to the roomy (2200 cu. in.) central compartment. Two small outside pockets are perfect for maps and other frequently used items. Two thousand JMP Travelers took these bags around the world last year and returned satisfied. Comparable bags cost much more. If you're looking for maximum "carry-on size" and a suitcase that can be converted into a back pack, this is your best bet. Available in navy blue, black, gray or burgundy.

Money Belt . . . . $8.95 postpaid

Required! Ultra-light, sturdy, under-the-pants, nylon pouch just big enough to carry the essentials comfortably. We never travel without one and hope you won't either. Beige, nylon zipper, one size fits all, with instructions.

Qty.	Title	Each	Total
	Alaska in 22 Days - *Lanier* (March '88)	$ 6.95	
	American Southwest in 22 Days - *Harris* (April '88)	6.95	
	Australia in 22 Days - *Gottberg*	6.95	
	China in 22 Days - *Duke & Victor*	6.95	
	Europe in 22 Days - *Steves*	6.95	
	Germany, Austria & Switzerland in 22 Days - *Steves*	6.95	
	Great Britain in 22 Days - *Steves*	6.95	
	India in 22 Days - *Mathur* (April '88)	6.95	
	Japan in 22 Days - *Old*	6.95	
	Mexico in 22 Days - *Rogers & Rosa*	6.95	
	Norway, Denmark & Sweden in 22 Days - *Steves*	6.95	
	West Indies in 22 Days - *Morreale*	6.95	
	All-Suite Hotel Guide - *Lanier*	9.95	
	Asia 101 - *Gottberg* (March '88)	11.95	
	Asia Through the Back Door - *Steves & Gottberg*	11.95	
	Complete Guide to Bed & Breakfasts - *Lanier*	12.95	
	Elegant Small Hotels - *Lanier*	12.95	
	Europe 101 - *Steves*	11.95	
	Europe Through the Back Door - *Steves*	11.95	
	Gypsying After 40 - *Harris*	12.95	
	Heart of Jerusalem - *Nellhaus* (Feb. '88)	12.95	
	Mona Winks - *Steves* (April '88)	9.95	
	People's Guide to Camping in Mexico - *Franz* (April '88)	11.95	
	People's Guide to Mexico - *Franz*	13.95	
		Subtotal	$
		Shipping	$ 1.75
		Total enclosed	$

Non-U.S. payments must be in
U.S. funds drawn on a U.S. bank.

METHOD OF PAYMENT (CHECK ONE)
[ ] Charge to my (circle one):   MasterCard   VISA   AmEx
[ ] Check or Money Order Enclosed (Sorry, no CODs or Cash)
Credit Card Number

Expiration Date ☐☐ — ☐☐

Signature _____
Required for Credit Card Purchases
Telephone: Office (___) _____ Home (___) _____
Name _____
Address _____
City _____ State _____ Zip _____

Send to: John Muir Publications
P.O. Box 613   Santa Fe, NM 87504-0613
(505) 982-4078
Please allow 4-6 weeks for delivery.